ARTIFICIAL INTELLIGENCE IN HEALTHCARE

The Impact of Digital Transformation and Big Data Analytics in Healthcare System

KOLLURI VENKATESWARANAIDU

ISBN 979-8-89699-187-8

DEDICATION

This book is dedicated to all my family members, especially to my parents who believed in me throughout my career. I would like to thank the researchers and scientists who inspired me for what I have become today

CONTENTS

Contents

GRATITUDE

Mr. Kolluri Venkateswaranaidu is a Senior Data Scientist / Architect who provides the design and architecture of the software systems and transforms the data. He holds a master's degree from US university and has around 10 years of work experience in Information technology, researcher, scholarly author, Leader and having extraordinary ability in the field of Information technology and especially in Artificial Intelligence, Machine Learning and Cyber Security. With his outstanding achievements as research scholar with multiple scholarly articles and other media publications recognised as a leader and his activities reflect a career of acclaimed work in the field.

Mr. Kolluri has written his first scholarly article titled "THE IMPACT OF DIGITAL TRANSFORMATION AND BIG DATA ANALYTICS IN HEALTHCARE SYSTEM" which is stepping stone to his research career, He has written numerous scholarly articles on how Artificial Intelligence and Machine learning is going to change the world of Health care, several media publication and fellow member in association who are recognized as nation and international associations/publications. Mr. Kolluri has worked in the field of Information technology especially Artificial Intelligence and Machine learning for years and has reached a point where he is a recognized as a highly respected leader in the varying industries associated with his field.

Mr. Kolluri ensure that he stays completely up to date with his fast-moving industry, thriving on living on the cutting edge of technology and being sufficiently advanced in this so as to be able to demonstrate his research and scholarly articles' experience and offer measured peer review to the journals where he has found a home on the board.

Mr. Kolluri was born and Lived in Ongole, Andhra Pradesh, a city he still loves. He now lives in Austin, Texas where he worked as Senior Data Scientist/ Architect. His Master's degree is from University of Mary Hardin Baylor with a focus in Information Systems and Technology which made him what he is today. His working life begin with App solutions Inc as Systems Analyst and this is mere stepping stone and this experience helped him to become a leader in his field.

When Mr. Kolluri isn't working, he spends time with the family and he loves to travel to explore the new culture and try new things in life. He also dreamed one day of passing along his passion for writing and his knowledge to future leaders in such a way that they would embrace new ideas and critical thinking in Artificial Intelligence and Machine Learning.

CHAPTER 1

Introduction to Artificial Intelligence in Healthcare

1.1 The Foundations of Artificial Intelligence in Healthcare

1.1.1 AI and Its Role in Medicine and key developmental milestone

The definition of artificial intelligence (AI) is "a branch of science and engineering concerned with the computational understanding of what is commonly called intelligent behaviour, and with the creation of artefacts that exhibit such behaviour." Through his syllogisms, a three-part deductive reasoning method, Aristotle sought to formalise "right thinking" (logic). This served as an inspiration for a lot of the work done in the modern age, and the early research on how the mind works contributed to the development of modern logical thinking. Artificial intelligence systems are programs that allow computers to behave in ways that mimic human intelligence. Among the pioneers of contemporary computer science and artificial intelligence was the British mathematician Alan Turing (1950). By defining intelligent behaviour in a computer as the capacity to complete cognitive tasks at a level comparable to that of a human, he created what became known as the "Turing test." Researchers have been investigating the possible uses of intelligent approaches in all areas of medicine since the middle of the previous century. When he looked into the idea of using computer analysis to diagnose severe abdominal discomfort in 1976, Gunn began the first series of investigations into the use of AI technology in surgery. Interest in medical AI has increased during the past 20 years (Athanasopoulou et al., 2022).

Acquiring, analysing, and using the vast quantity of knowledge required to address intricate clinical issues is a difficulty for modern medicine. The creation of AI applications meant to assist clinicians in diagnosing patients, choosing treatments, and forecasting results has been linked to the growth of medical artificial intelligence. They are made to help healthcare professionals with tasks that need the manipulation of information and data in their daily work. These systems include hybrid intelligent systems, fuzzy expert systems, evolutionary computation, and artificial neural networks (ANNs) (Huang et al., 2023)

Artificial neural networks

The number of publications over the past 20 years indicates that ANN is the most widely used AI method in medicine. An analogy of the biological nervous system, artificial neural networks (ANNs) are computational analytical tools. They are made up of "neurones," which are networks of highly connected computer processors that can process data and express knowledge in parallel. Their capacity to handle imprecise information, analyse non-linear data, generalise, and learn from past examples has made them a very desirable analytical tool in the medical profession. This allows the model to be used to independent data.

The first artificial neurone was created by McCulloch and Pitts in 1943 using basic binary threshold functions. The Perceptron, a useful model created by psychologist Frank Rosenblatt in 19588, was the next significant turning point. The multilayer feedforward Perceptron (Fig. 1.1) has been the most often used model of the fundamental Perceptron network, but numerous modifications have been presented. The layers of neurones that make up these networks are usually an input layer, one or more middle or hidden layers, and an output layer. All of these levels are completely coupled to every other layer. There is a numerical weight assigned to each link that connects the neurones. By making these weight adjustments repeatedly, a neural network "learns." Learning from experience in a training environment is one of the key characteristics of ANNs. Before Paul Werbos, a PhD student, proposed "backpropagation" learning in 1974, the application of multilayer feedforward perceptron's was limited by the absence of an appropriate learning algorithm. Other well-liked network designs include the Self-organising Feature Map, Hopfield networks, and Radial Basis Function.

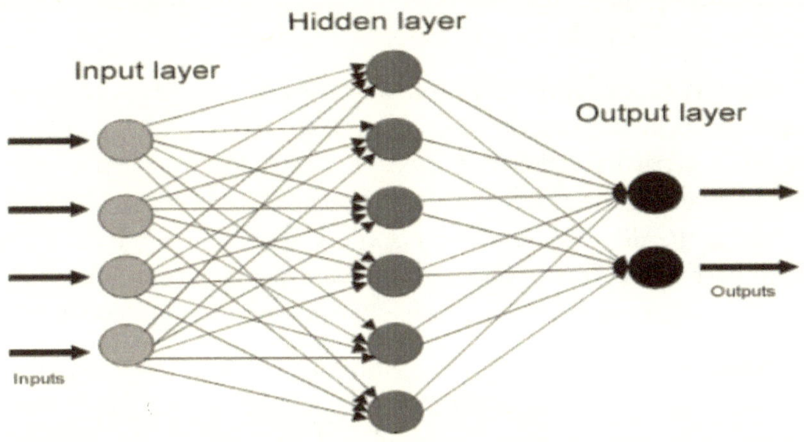

Figure 1.1: Multi-layered feedforward artificial neural networks.

Source: - (Kirişci, 2019)

In the actual world, ANNs have already been used in many different contexts. Their accuracy in pattern recognition and classification has drawn researchers to use them to address a variety of therapeutic issues. The need for analytical tools like artificial neural networks (ANNs) that can take advantage of the complex relationships between various clinical, biological, and pathological variables is increasing as we realise that diagnosis, treatment, and outcome prediction in many clinical situations depend on a complex interaction of these variables.

Baxt was among the first scientists to investigate ANNs' potential for clinical use. He created a neural network model that correctly identified acute myocardial infarction and later confirmed his findings prospectively with comparable precision. ANNs have since been used in practically every area of medicine.

ANNs have been applied to waveform analysis, data interpretation in critical care settings, image analysis in radiology and histology, and clinical diagnosis.

Prostates can be benign or cancerous, and this test utilizes a neural network classification method called the Prost sure Index developed by Stamey et al., (1996). Originally developed, this model was subsequently assessed in prospective trials, achieving a diagnostic accuracy ranging from 90%, sensitivity from 81% and specificity from 92%. ANNs can be also applied for glaucoma, back pain, retained common bile duct stones, abdominal discomfort and appendicitis and other surgically relevant disorders.

Different wave shapes have been investigated through ANNs' pattern recognition, including signal wave from ECG for diagnosing ventricular arrhythmias, atrial fibrillation, and myocardial infarction. Application of neural networks involving the analysis of electro-encephalogram (EEG) has enabled their use in the diagnosis of sleep disorders and epilepsy. Moreover, they claim to have learnt how to interpret electromyography (EMG) wave forms and Doppler ultrasonography and haemodynamic patterns in the critically ill.

In order to plan the treatment approaches and the follow-up, accurate prognosis is inevitable. These populations could be precisely identified for intensified adjuvant treatment, which would cure the illness and prolong survival. Due to the nature of algorithm ANNs can effectively analyze complex cancer data as they do not require linear correlation of the variables. In patients with colorectal and breast cancer, neural networks have been shown to be able to predict survival. When it comes to forecasting the prognosis of patients with colorectal cancer, ANNs have also demonstrated superior performance versus consultant colorectal surgeons.

Fuzzy expert systems

The science of reasoning, inference, and thinking that acknowledges and applies the reality that everything is a matter of degree is known as fuzzy logic. Fuzzy logic acknowledges that most things would actually lie somewhere in between, that is, in different shades of grey, as opposed to conventional logic, which assumes everything is black and white. Lofty Zadeh, a University of California engineer, popularised it in 1965.[46] Unlike Boolean or conventional logic, which employs sharp differences, i.e., 0 for false and 1 for true, it uses continuous set membership from 0 to 1. Since medicine is basically a continuous field, the majority of medical data are by nature imprecise. Medical applications benefit greatly from fuzzy logic, a data handling paradigm that allows for ambiguity. It effectively leverages and captures the idea of fuzziness in a computational way. "Medical diagnostics and, to a lesser extent, the description of biological systems are the most likely areas of application for this theory," Zadeh stated in 1969.[47] The structure of fuzzy expert systems is a set of "if-then" modelling rules.

Numerous medical applications have investigated fuzzy logic approaches. Schneider et al. demonstrated that when employing tumour marker profiles to diagnose lung cancer, fuzzy logic outperformed multiple logistic regression analysis. Likewise, the use of fuzzy logic has been investigated in the diagnosis of pancreatic, breast, and acute leukaemia. Additionally, they have been used to characterise MRI images of brain tumours, liver lesions on ultrasound and CT scans, and breast ultrasound images. Another application of fuzzy logic is the prediction of survival for breast cancer patients. In order to regulate blood pressure during the perioperative phase, fuzzy controllers have been developed for the administration of vasodilators. In the operating room, they have also been utilised to administer anaesthetics.

Evolutionary computation

The term "evolutionary computation" refers to a broad range of computing methods that mimic the survival of the fittest and natural selection processes in real-world problem-solving. "Genetic algorithms" are the type of evolutionary computation most frequently utilised in medical applications. A class of stochastic search and optimisation algorithms based on spontaneous biological evolution was proposed by John Holland in 1975. They operate by coming up with numerous arbitrary answers to the given issue. After that, this population of several options will develop from one generation to the next until the issue is satisfactorily resolved. By eliminating the subpar answers, the best ones are added to the population. If this process is repeated among the better elements, the population will continue to progress, survive, and come up with new solutions.

A search in a vast and complicated space can be used to formulate the majority of medical decisions. When evaluating a cytological material to determine whether or not it is malignant, for instance, a cytologist looks for a collection of characteristics that will allow him to make a definitive diagnosis. Natural evolution's mechanism is used by genetic algorithms to search a given space efficiently. Numerous functions, including planning and scheduling, medical imaging and signal processing, diagnosis and prognosis, and more, are carried out by them. The concepts of genetic algorithms have been applied to the prediction of outcomes in cases of melanoma, lung cancer, critically ill patients, and warfarin response. They have also been utilised in computerised mammography microcalcification analysis, brain tumour MRI segmentation to assess the effectiveness of treatment approaches64, and computerised 2-D image analysis to identify malignant melanomas.

Hybrid intelligent systems

Every AI method has pros and cons of its own. Evolutionary computation with search and optimisation, fuzzy logic with imprecision, and learning are the primary concerns of neural networks. Combining the benefits of these technologies can result in hybrid intelligent systems that complement one another. Their combined effect enables a hybrid system to use human-like reasoning mechanisms, deal with imprecision and ambiguity, accommodate common sense, extract knowledge from raw data, and learn to adapt to an unfamiliar and quickly changing environment. Although there are many other hybrid systems accessible, the most widely used ones include genetic algorithms for automatically training and creating neural network architectures, ANNs for developing fuzzy systems, and fuzzy systems for designing ANNs. The use of hybrid intelligent systems has once more been investigated in a wide range of therapeutic settings. Examples include the detection of coronary artery stenosis, the examination of microcalcification on digital mammograms, the diagnosis of breast cancer, the evaluation of cardiac viability, and the regulation of anaesthesia depth (Seera & Lim, 2014).

1.1.2 Differentiating Between Machine Learning, Deep Learning, and AI

Artificial Intelligence (AI) serves as an umbrella term encompassing a range of technologies designed to simulate human intelligence in machines. Within this broad domain, Machine Learning (ML) and Deep Learning (DL) represent specialized subsets, each contributing uniquely to the transformative impact of AI in healthcare. Understanding the distinctions among these terms is crucial for comprehending their applications in the healthcare landscape.

AI involves the creation of models and programs effective in solving problems that were originally solved by human brain in matters including but not limited to understanding, analysis, and even decision. From diagnosis to simple automation of administrative processes, we see the use of AI in the healthcare sector. However, AI includes several approaches, and the two dominants are ML and DL, which contribute to the progress of the former.

Artificial Intelligence is a broad field of study and one of the subcategories within AI is Machine Learning that deals with providing computers the ability to improve on their performance when exposed to data without being programmed on what they found out. Machine learning is a learning process in which an ML model aims at establishing relationships between datasets and make predictions regarding the same. For example, in the healthcare sector, it is used for developing disease prediction models, risk assessment of patient and forecasting of outcomes of treatments. Some of the important algorithms used in ML include; decision trees, support vector machines, and random forest. These models work well with ordered data and also for these models, there is a need to assign the input variables for the model to train from, a process known as feature selection.

The other classification is called Deep Learning, which is a complex form of ML that uses artificial neural network, which is modeled, like the brain of a human being. DL algorithms select features on their own from raw data hence removing the burden of feature selection. This capability makes DL especially useful in working with large datasets of high-dimensionality for which applications include medical images, genomic sequencing data, and unstructured data such as clinical narratives. In healthcare, DL is in a position to perform relatively well particularly in areas such as determination of human image such as for diagnosis of diseases through radiology, pathology or dermatology where accuracy is almost similar to that of qualified doctors. CNNs, RNNs, and GANs are the most widely used types of DL architectures used in these domains.

However, for creating models, although ML models are known to work effectively with labeled data, they necessitate a small dataset, whereas DL tends to coax into scenarios with big data and unstructured information. But challenges are there as DL uses massive computational infrastructure and another limitation of DL is that it's a 'black box,' meaning one cannot understand its decisioning process easily. As for the limitations, for most cases, the ML models are more explainable and computationally less intensive for most applications requiring such features (Janiesch et al., 2021).

Integrating ML and DL with other AI categories has greatly impacted the health care delivery system across the world. Whereas ML models have been most used to prescriptive functions such as predictive analytics in electronic health record (EHRs), deep learning has made it possible to revolutionize precision medicine and real-time data monitoring via wearable technology. All these technologies put in the hand of clinician's tools that aid the diagnostic accuracy, treatment planning and overall outcome of care.

In summary, AI is the broad concept of building human-like intelligent machines, while ML and DL are massive subfields within the AI umbrella. The feature selection in ML requires structured data and human interference, in contrast, DL contains deep neural networks for the consideration of large-volume datasets. Although we see more and more adoption of AI-based solutions in the healthcare industry, it is critical to understand the differences and interactions between AI, ML, DL.

1.2 The Digital Transformation of the Healthcare Industry

Interest in automation is growing as a result of rising healthcare expenditures. It should be mentioned, although, that in certain medical fields, such as medicines or assistive automation in surgery, which permits operations beyond human capabilities (micro surgeries, for example), automation is sought to provide higher quality. A major digital revolution is occurring in surgery, as diagnostic techniques provide data that is automatically analysed to create a model that is used to simulate procedures and eventually employed by autonomous or semi-autonomous surgical systems (Hermes et al., 2020).

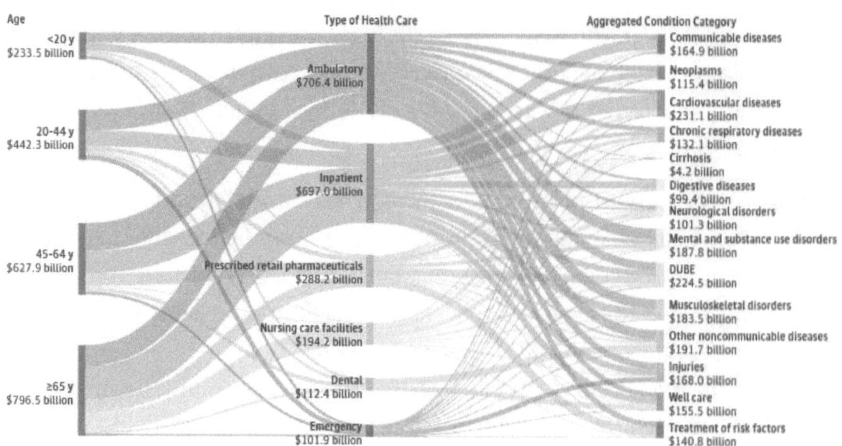

Figure 1.2:   Personal Health Care Spending in the United States by Age Group, Aggregated Condition Category, and Type of Health Care, 2013

Source: - (Dieleman et al., 2016)

1.2.1 Overview of Digital Technologies in Patient Care

The entire healthcare industry is changing due to the digital revolution, which is also altering how people view the field. Evidently, symbiotic autonomous systems are also beginning to appear in the healthcare industry, primarily in the form of intelligent prostheses.

Several autonomous systems applications are linked to the digital transformation of health care, falling under three primary areas of disruption.

Healthcare Delocalization

Because autonomous systems can help on-site, they are beginning to contribute to the delocalisation of care. The fact that this began in controlled settings like hospitals and care centres is not surprising, but it is now spreading to home-care (Singh, 2018).

Examples of autonomous robots include those that prepare and deliver medications to patients in a hospital ward and those that clean rooms, such as those made by Xenex, which are used in hospitals, long-term care facilities, and homes with elderly people who are vulnerable to infections (Terry, 2019)neither model seems particularly appropriate for regulating machines practicing medicine or the complex man-machine relationships that will develop. Additionally, healthcare AI will join other technologies such as big data and mobile health apps in highlighting current deficiencies in healthcare regulatory models, particularly in data protection. The article first suggests a typology for healthcare AI technologies based in large part of their potential for substituting for humans and follows with a critical examination of the existing healthcare regulatory mechanisms (device regulation, licensure, privacy and confidentiality, reimbursement, market forces, and litigation.

ABB established a research centre on the grounds of the Texas Medical Centre Innovation complex in Houston in October 2019. The creation of autonomous robots for use in healthcare in a hospital setting is its primary goal. These robots, known as cobots, are made to cooperate and function independently as a group.

Within the Texas Medical Centre Innovation site in Houston, ABB established a research centre in October 2019. In order to provide healthcare in a hospital setting, it is initially concentrating on the creation of autonomous robots. Known as cobots, these robots are made to cooperate and function independently as a group.

Although they are being researched in a number of research institutes, fully autonomous robots that can conduct surgery in remote areas are not yet operational. There are currently robots that can be controlled remotely and have a restricted range of autonomy. By utilising its low latency, which can facilitate (to a limited extent) the use of haptic feedback, 5G, the next generation of communications networks, has frequently been associated with enabling remote surgery utilising an onsite robot. There have been a few trials of autonomous robots, such as the one at Boston Children Hospital where medical professionals repaired a heart valve by using an autonomous micro-robot to explore inside the body.

In the upcoming ten years, more areas are probably going to be investigated, such as suturing automation. Surgical robots have been using artificial intelligence (AI) in a variety of ways to improve their awareness and decision-making skills during the past year. Legal concerns are obviously important in this field, namely, who is accountable for a robot's autonomous judgements and the results of its operation?

Healthcare Personalization

Genome sequencing has become a mass commercial reality. Since 2016, the price had been falling but had stayed steady at about $1000. In the upcoming ten years, it is anticipated that the cost will begin to decline once more due to improved mapping technologies (using machine learning, which is getting better as more genomes are sequenced and mapped). Businesses like Illumina, a global leader in sequencing, Nebula Genomics, Zenome, and DNA tix are using blockchain technology to map genomic data, making it accessible and likely to take over in the next ten years, lowering the cost of premium services. However, other businesses that cater to the mass market today, like as 23AndMe and Ancestry, offer limited sequencing for less than $100, and as the number of genomes they have sequenced increases, they are quickly increasing their capacity for mapping and sequencing. Over the next ten years, we can anticipate that these two forces—one from the top and the other from the bottom—will significantly alter how genetics is used in healthcare.

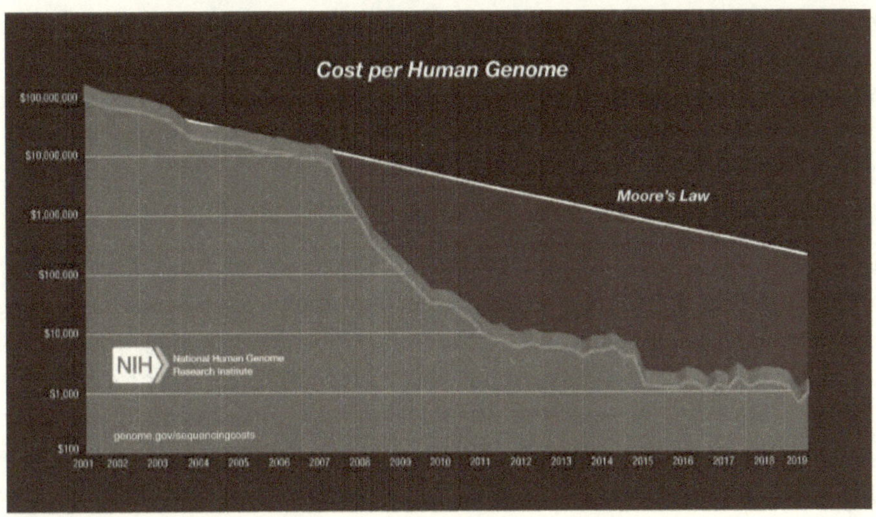

Figure 1.3:   The falling price of sequencing the entire human genome. Human Genome Research Institute (NIH)

Source: - (Rowe & Lester, 2020)

Confusion over the various numbers related to genome sequencing is one issue of the modern era, such as:

- The amount of storage needed for a human genome ranges from 3GB (one byte is equivalent to one base pair) to up to 200 TB, which is the massive amount of data that results from the parallel sequencing of the millions of DNA fragments, with some amounts in the hundreds of GB range to preserve the unmapped DNA strings;

- The cost of deciphering the genome can range from $850 for sequencing to $3,000 for mapping the genome (converting the strings of nucleotides A-C-G-T to genes) and much more to comprehend gene expression;

- The cost of locating a certain gene, or something that defines a conventional procedure for curing a particular type of cancer.

Precision medicine, which is another word for personalisation, is gaining popularity as a result of falling costs and more data becoming available, which supports predictive analytics and makes more advanced AI possible. In an effort to establish a genetic biobank, the Obama administration started the Precision Medicine Initiative, which has since evolved into the All of Us initiative1. In order to create a genome bank that is expanding by 235,000 Whole Genome Sequences (WGS) annually, France is actively working on the "France Medecine Genomique 2025."

Personalized Healthcare / Digital Twins

In an effort to assist personalised medicine, businesses such as GE and Philips are investing in the development of a person's digital twin at the same time that our understanding and use of the human genome has improved. Digital twins are already being used to mimic hospitals, equipment, and processes, but they are also being viewed from the standpoint of proactive medicine more generally in relation to patients (Rivera et al., 2020)however, demands new and innovative methods for engineering systems that support the required capabilities. Research on the application of the novel concept of Digital Twin (DT.

The traditional healthcare business, including GE, Philips, Siemens, and Nokia, see digital twins in personal healthcare as a means of improving healthcare quality and lowering costs by leveraging data gathered from their equipment. They are also perceived—though this is not widely known—as a means of protecting themselves against the competitive assault from data-driven businesses that view digital twins as a means of leveraging their data and breaking into the healthcare market. This new generation of businesses is led by Google and Apple, with other companies like 23andMe, which have already been noted, attempting to profit from their data's accessibility.

In the battle between the "incumbents" and the "data companies," there probably won't be a clear winner for the first part of the upcoming decade, but the players will likely speed up the adoption of digital twins.

A significant thing to note is the anticipated development of digital twins to stage 4, at which a digital twin may function as an independent system and roam the internet using data and services to give its physical twin a personalised health advisory. There are already some indications that this evolution is going to happen soon; the Apple Watch 5 is one step in that direction, albeit on a relatively small healthcare market. It's anticipated that digital twins in healthcare will develop into independent systems that enable sophisticated, individualised treatment by the middle of the following decade.

Healthcare Digitalization – Leveraging Data

The whole healthcare system in many nations is either already digital or in the process of becoming so. Digitalisation is often, if not always, divided into distinct digital silos. Both radiography and blood test results are digital, but they are not publicly available, and relationships between them are frequently difficult. The largest obstacle to the digitalisation of healthcare is not so much digitising the individual components as it is bringing them together to form a cohesive whole. This problem is either organisational or technical. The second problem involves overcoming privacy and legal considerations in order to enable the analysis of data from various patients. However, if we are to take advantage of the digitalisation of healthcare, both obstacles must be addressed (Aerts & Bogdan-Martin, 2021)new digital technology provides tools to more effectively address the growing dual burden of disease. Two-thirds of the world's population subscribed to mobile services by the end of 2018, while the falling price of connectivity and the 5G networks rollout promise to accelerate the use of digital technology. Properly leveraged, we can employ digital solutions and applications to transform health systems from reactive to proactive and even preventive, helping people stay healthy. With artificial intelligence (AI.

The scheme in data leverage is the same here as it is in any other areas:

What is happening? - The patient's genome, metabolome, environment, occupation, activities and habits (such as travel, frequency, and habits like smoking, drinking, veganism, and getting a tan), and patient data (such as medical examinations, drug use, and data from wearable technology) can all be included in the data collected. The symptoms can be recognised and explained by connecting all of this information. All of these people's data can be organised into a digital twin of them, which the healthcare system and doctors can utilise as a middleman.

Why it is happening? - The same information mentioned above can also be used to diagnose: is it a virus infection that is genuinely spreading throughout a community or something that was contracted while travelling overseas, is it air pollution that is affecting the airways and causing an allergic reaction, is it the result of a treatment that is currently being administered and causing unwanted side effects, etc.

What might happen? - In light of the current condition, the patient's history, and their specifics, what might happen if nothing is done? What might happen to those that interact with that individual as well? In healthcare, there are typically a number of potential outcomes that must be assessed rather than just one. Depending on the condition and the situation, one is more likely than the others. Controlling potential epidemics is another issue to be assessed under this "what might happen" framework, which entails taking a step back from the patient to think about the bigger picture.

What can be done to change the outcome? Finding the best treatment or preventative steps to stop the spread is the key here. As was already mentioned, healthcare is becoming more individualised, which clearly includes identifying medications that are right for a given individual. Healthcare is moving towards the design of specific protocols that are focussing on the specificity of the patient, as opposed to the "one size fits them all" approach to curing that has been used for the past century. This approach was based on years and years of testing drugs on animals and then selecting patients through trials. In this approach, cancer remedies are being investigated and will gain much more attention in the years to come.

Since remedies will no longer be dependent on drawn-out studies but rather on a patient's specifics, this is probably going to cause a stir among the major pharmaceutical companies. Consequently, there is a need for constant, or nearly constant, monitoring. While the latter attracts tech firms developing wearables, implants, and ambient monitoring systems, the former opens the door to several businesses that can capitalise on the uniqueness of a field and whose strength is in data processing (machine learning and AI in general).

Healthcare Digitization – Chatbots

In many nations, the Electronic Health Record (EHR), which records patient information, is now a reality. A proposition for the exchange of HER throughout Europe has been endorsed by the European Community. However, take note that this advice permits a European national to make his electronic health record (EHR) accessible to any physician or hospital in the EU in the event that it becomes necessary. The data is not meant to be made available for intelligence or research purposes.

Since there isn't a single, widely recognised standard and each kind of EHR is dependent on the particular software provider, the situation is much more complicated in the US, where there are almost 700 distinct EHR implementations. Many times, doctors use an Electronic Medical Record (EMR) rather than an EHR to track a particular aspect of their practice.

For instance, each specialist may have an EMR of a patient that contains their unique information, but none of them can access the EMR created by the other doctors.

In order to develop a practical approach to using health data for research, the European Union supported a study in Europe called Electronic Health Record for Clinical Research (EHR4C). The privacy issues still make the implementation difficult. However, some bottom-up strategies, such as the one recently revealed by Apple, could put pressure on governments to develop and adopt a top-down data sharing solution. There is no question in the scientific world that a complete digital transition that makes hundreds of millions of people's health data available would greatly expand scientific knowledge and lead to incredible advancements in healing and public health.

- An autonomous "bot" can use the availability of people's health data to: Find trends, such as the onset of epidemics, harmful elements in an environment, the long-term effects of different environmental circumstances, etc.

- Offer individualised consultation services via chatbots, a "doctor on demand." Chatbots have been developed by hospitals and insurance companies to serve as interfaces for patients to access medical expertise. These include things like helping patients remember to take their medications (like the Florence chatbot), better understanding symptoms (like YourMD chatbot, which is already installed in a few million smartphones), and helping with diagnosis (like Sensely chatbot, which is a service offered by insurance and pharmaceutical companies).

- Help doctors diagnose and develop a cure, similar to Unanimous AI's services where bots scour the internet's health knowledge space and give clinicians the most recent information.

It's intriguing to note that chatbots can improve healthcare in places where resources and geography (remote areas) restrict access to care. Undoubtedly, this can happen anywhere in the globe, but there may be drawbacks, as noted in Robin Cook2's medical thriller Cell, which explores the impact of chatbots on the medical field and how they affect pharmaceutical and medical insurance firms.

1.2.2 Success Stories of Digital Transformation in Leading Institutions

The digital revolution is causing a significant upheaval in the healthcare industry. Previously centred on in-person meetings and paper documentation, this sector is currently using digital tools and technology more and more to enhance patient care and operational effectiveness. The fantastic capability of digital transformation in healthcare is emerging through more success stories, where many leaders agree on charts to watch to map out the journey.

- ***Case Study 1: The case of using predictive analytics in Johns Hopkins Hospital in Baltimore, Maryland***

Starting the process of digital transformation, the well-known brand in the context of healthcare was Johns Hopkins Hospital that used predictive analytics. The hospital aimed at reducing readmissions that are common and increase medical costs as well as being an indication of poor care or discharge.

To analyse patient data, and to anticipate potential readmissions the hospital integrated a predictive analytics program into its setup. Demographic information, vital statistics, previous diseases, and the type of disease in which a patient is ill – all this the model takes into consideration. The outcomes have been revolutionary: readmissions have reduced meaningfully at the Johns Hopkins reducing patient's health complications and costs.

- ***Case Study 2: Mayo Clinic (Rochester, Minnesota) – Embracing Telemedicine***

The use of telemedicine by the Mayo Clinic is another quite vivid example of the process going digital. One of the challenges that exist in the health care industry was handling with patient's care especially those who reside in remote areas was addressed by the Mayo Clinic via digital technology.

Amongst the services that they provide they have a complete telemedicine solution that contains digital diagnosis, remote monitoring, and video conferencing. It was huge, for the simple reason that it enabled the Mayo Clinic to treat patients who earlier could not manage to get to the clinic due to distances. Besides the promotion of the accessibility to the healthcare, the presented digital strategy has positively impacted on the patients' satisfaction and health.

- ***Case Study 3: Kaiser Permanente: Promoting Electronic Health Records in Oakland, California***

Kaiser Foundation, the largest healthcare provider made history by going fully paperless by adopting Electronic Health Records (EHRs). EHRs convert patient information into digital form which is convenient and significantly increases provider to provider communication.

The digital change has improved patient care because healthcare providers can now have full access to a patient's history, current prescriptions, and even test results. The change to EHRs was also a positive aspect of reducing time and work, where physicians and their patients saved time from removing many tests and administrative works that add no value.

1.3 Big Data Analytics: A Pillar of Modern Healthcare

Big data analytics has emerged as a transformative force in modern healthcare, offering unprecedented opportunities to analyse vast and diverse datasets to improve patient outcomes, optimize healthcare delivery, and advance medical research. The incorporation of Electronic Health Records (EHRs), genomic data, and wearable devices has made big data analytics as one of the key drivers of current healthcare advancement (Palanisamy & Thirunavukarasu, 2019).

Electronic health records (EHRs) is among the most important sources of data in the big data analytics. EHR captures detailed and continuous patient information including patients' demographics, health history, laboratory and diagnostic test results, treatment plan and outcomes. This abundant source of structured and unstructured data also enables the generation of effective models for the disease management, population at risk and treatment decision making. For instance, EHR data analyzed can reveal patterns in chronic illnesses or identify the risk factors for deterioration, and subsequent action can be taken promptly. In addition, EHRs serve to support organizational functioning related to decrease of readmission rates or efficient distribution of funds. Another important type of data that has made its way to the world of big data analytics is genomic data. Recent innovations in NGS have brought enormous amounts of genomic data, factors that have precipitated personalized medicine. Big data analysis enables the connection of genomic data with clinical data in order to identify genes linked to diseases and create individual genetic treatment plans. For example, pharmacogenomic studies anticipate patient reactions toward drugs to achieve better therapeutic outcomes with less side effects. Furthermore, data derived from the genome plays a role in early diagnosis of inherited disorders, identification of specific treatments, and delineation of disease processes at the molecular level.

Mobile health is already extending the concepts of big data in healthcare by offering constant; measuring of physiological indices through devices such as fitness trackers, smartwatches, and medical sensors. Metrics which are collected through wearables include heart rate, blood pressure, glucose level and activity patterns. These data streams provide tools to healthcare providers to monitor patient health status apart from face-to-face meetings, improve the management of chronic diseases, and focus more attention on prevention. For instance, wearing devices can notify the patient and the doctors of high or low levels of glucose in the body and take corrective measures before hospitalization and high expenses on health. In addition, large-scale data generated by wearables are suitable for epidemiological research and health system policymaking.

1.4 Transforming Patient Outcomes Through AI

1.4.1 Using AI for Faster and More Accurate Diagnostics

Advancements in technology have shifted the operational and business paradigms at a very fast pace and the healthcare industry is arguably at the vanguard of this evolution. The growing focus on patient centrality in care delivery introduces the application of Artificial Intelligence and Machine Learning into the predictive healthcare space. Being capable of processing big amounts of data, these innovative technologies equip clinicians with a set of abilities to predict the patient's results, increase the efficiency of diagnosis, and individualize the therapy. This essay will analyst how AI and ML changing the landscapes of the healthcare by discussing the possibilities they offered from early diagnosis of the diseases to manage the resources for patients and for healthcare facilities impactfully. Finally, there is a need to grasp and utilize those technologies for both better patients' prognosis and more effective organization of healthcare system from the view point of its contribution to the society. Increased adoption of AI and ML in healthcare is transforming the experience of physicians, care givers and ultimately patients. These technologies can analyze big data, including patient's medical records, observation of the same patient and even other patients in real time, and come up with elaborate patterns, and predictive models with very high accuracy. AI supported instruments help clinicians diagnose diseases in the preliminary stages, which may sometimes remain undiscovered by the naked human eye. In addition, the results of this study can be utilized to further personalize treatment plans—through the use of machine learning algorithms—which adjust therapies to an individual's genetic profile and prior experiences with cancer treatments. This strategy of precision medicine does not only improve the effectiveness of treatment but there is also little chance of having side effects. Moreover, AI and ML help review and improve the efficiency of the healthcare delivery systems by minimizing the utilization of resources, time, and effort as well as improving the management of patients.

1.4.2 Role of Predictive Analytics in Preventing Diseases

The use of artificial intelligence (AI) and machine learning (ML) into the analysis of predictive health analytics is among the major breakthroughs in the health sector as it improves the patient's prognosis by enabling early actions to be taken. These technologies make use of large sample of data to predict and recognize probable health risks that will aid the clinician in decision making. For example, modern artificial intelligence systems apply predictive analysis to improve patient flows during the perioperative period as some studies suggest how such systems can help estimate surgical times and reduce patient waits. Moreover, with the development of the fifth generation of networks, the possibility of working in real time with data is becoming more and more realistic, which will enable prompt reaction to patient's requirements and better cooperation between the healthcare professionals. This convergence of advanced technologies such as AI, ML and next generation of connectivity not only brings solution to already existing archaic model of healthcare delivery systems but also opens gateway for a more innovative, proactive, patient centric model of delivering care.

The incorporation of the predictive models into the health care systems reflects a paradigm shift towards improvement of the overarching health care delivery system through proactive patient management. AI algorithms enable the healthcare providers to analyze and subsequently predict instances of the possible outbreaks of health complications, always allowing measures to be taken in advance. For example, using accurate inputs on patient history, it is possible to diagnose chronic diseases before they advance; this means patients will receive the correct treatment to improve their health. Moreover, as underscored by the literature, the utilization of AI will enhance the delivery of care by customizing approaches of care delivery through strategic information from the patient's data. Furthermore, the integration of multiple novel technologies, including IoT and big data, generates an environment for constant monitoring of patient status, leading toward the improvement of precision medicine. This integration not only improves the quality of patient care also empowers a future-proof healthcare environment.

Predictive modeling for early disease detection

Predictive modeling is a new area that offers a lot in early diagnosis of diseases and helps the health care professionals to see possible health complications before they occur. These models improve both diagnosis and treatment by integrating data from sociodemographic and clinical data, as well as data acquired from neuroimaging studies. For example, use of AI and ML makes it possible to evaluate intricate data and enhance the chances of patients with neurocognitive disorders. In addition, analytics applied in Intensive Care Units (ICUs) provides practical values on resource utilizations and patients' management, has major positive effects on the conditions of the critically ill patients. The application of predictive modeling will gradually become more and more significant for, not only, identifying the conditions at the early stage but also for developing appropriate treatment plans and thus, changing the paradigm in the delivery of healthcare and promoting early preventive approach to health.

Personalized treatment plans based on predictive analytics

It is potential of the predictive analytics that is highly significant for the healthcare industry to move from the traditional 'one size fits all' model of care plans. With the help of various sorts of patient data – genetic, lifestyle, and environmental – doctors and other healthcare professionals can develop treatment regimens that are most effective for each patient. They are AI and ML that look into large amounts of data in a bid to identify patterns and potential patient response to certain therapies and have over time enhanced this particular approach. Some of the data points to the fact that when clinical decisions are made using AI-predictive modelling the effectiveness is not only gained in terms of efficiency but also appropriateness in the implementation of individualized patient care. Therefore, as stated in the Smart Healthcare initiative, the process through application of AI and analytics is to adapt in real time due to the availability of systems and a better health care experience for the patient that is stronger and more tailored for the individual. It means that there occurred the shift toward more proactive and patient-centered model of care. Advancements in the use of analytics, where a patient's personal details including genetic makeup, lifestyle predispositions and environmental factors can be incorporated into a patient's individual prescription are driving this trend towards more personalized medicine. AI, as well as ML, allows an ability among healthcare professionals to explore large datasets and to define trends on how patients will respond to specific therapies. This makes treatment more accurate, specific to a patient, and also enhances the outcome of treatment and the level of compliance. The Smart Healthcare initiative show that by transforming the clinical decision-making using AI tools and predictive analysis, treatment plans can be adjusted in real-time as suggested by the change in the risk scores which will make healthcare going forward more proactive and patient centric. This evolution presents a intriguing shift from old conventional approaches based on more conventional one approach that fits for all to a more flexible and individualistic approach to health care delivery, with the possibility of enhanced results.

Impact on patient engagement and adherence to treatment

Effective patient participation and drug compliance are revolutionized where the use of artificial intelligence, and machine learning is incorporated in the medical field. Computerized tools for communication that are based on artificial intelligence allow medical workers to adapt the conversation within the context of treatment, individualizing the experience in order to increase compliance. For instance, the real-time observation of patients' vital signs is driven by IoMT systems that feed data into the network. This not only educates the patients but also empowers them by engaging them in their health care. Furthermore, the use of the Explainable AI system could improve patient trust because the system provides information on the decisions made regarding prioritization or recommendations on patient treatment at every level of the care delivery system, which can only increase patient confidence in their care. Finally, through integration of these innovative technologies, not only is compliance enhanced but also the patients are put at central stage of their health management hence better health and high satisfaction levels.

1.4.3 Personalized Medicine and Its Potential Impact on Patient Care

Personalized medicine or precision medicine is another innovative form of medicine delivery system that seeks to deliver medical interventions that are specific to a patient's characteristics. This is in contrast to the traditional approach to practice where treatment and service are developed with little reference to the patient's unique attributes. Thanks to the wealth of information with regards to an individual's genetic make-up, his/her immediate environment and lifestyle, tailored medicine makes highly informed decisions when it comes to diagnosis, prognosis and treatment plans. This is why individualized medicine is one of the most important trends in modern healthcare; it allows creating effective treatment regimens with fewer side effects and changes the paradigm of patient treatment in cases of diseases.

In the diagnosis, treatment planning and patient care management, artificial intelligence greatly transformed the healthcare industry. Nowadays, due to the application of AI technologies, the whole potential of personalized medicine can be implemented because the artificial intelligence is capable of working with and analyzing large amounts of data at a speed unprecedented before. They are great at pattern recognition in big data like genomics, imaging and EHRs which are too large for a human to process. AI with its features of machine learning as well as deep learning algorithms provides new solutions to numerous problems in the field of healthcare, beginning from better diagnostics and prognosis of a patient's condition, and ending with individual recommendations regarding further treatment. These following AI Technologies in Personalized Medicine-

Data Analysis and Interpretation

Artificial Intelligence is now a fundamental tool in the assessment and understanding of the multifaceted and comprehensive biological data that hold the key to the philosophy of personalized medicine. In large datasets of genotypic and phenotypic information, EHRs, and biomedical imaging, AI can parse relationships beyond the capacity of conventional analysis. Machine learning models which are a subcategory of AI algorithms, are extremely suited for analyzing the subtle of genomics. These models may estimate thresholds of disease, interpret genetic predisposition and even predict the disease progression based on the subject's genome. This kind of direct communication allows the development of highly individualistic strategies, as healthcare providers have the patient's complete genomic profile at their disposal. The ability of the AI in the prediction of disease risks based on the genetic data improves the reliability of the model. It creates new opportunities for the concept of preventive medicine, which can be made when a particular disease has not yet appeared.

Diagnostic Tools

The use of Artificial Intelligence in diagnosing diseases is a step up to the improvement of the diagnostic tools in terms of accuracy and duration.

Standard clinical examinations that rely on personal estimation of medical pictures and tests, are intrinsically prone to error and inconsistency. This is the reason why AI systems excel at expounding complicated diagnostic data consistently and objectively including high-resolution scans or elaborate symptoms. For instance, deep learning algorithms have beating human medical diagnoses in diseases such as cancer, diabetic retinopathy, and cardiovascular diseases by analyzing medical images in the best way that no human sight can ever do. These AI based diagnostics shorten the time from symptom onset to diagnosis and increase the confidence placed in those diagnoses which in turn allows for earlier and more precise action to be taken.

Treatment Planning and Predictions

AI also has a role in the treatment's planning and prognosis, in order to improve and develop personalized treatment plans. Machine algorithms can predict the possible response of a patient to a given set of drugs or therapy regimens using multiple informants including genetic makeup, patient's history, and previous treatment outcome. This capability is especially useful in oncology; the produced AI models can indicate the proper course of chemotherapy drugs for a patient while also taking into account the side effects, all derived from the tumor's genetic profile. Furthermore, AI can predict how drugs might interact with each other, or cause side effects, which are other ways of personalizing treatment to be not only effective but safe. AI's future perspectives also define the treatment outcomes and improve the quality of patient's life, reducing detrimental side effects.

Wearable Technology and Remote Monitoring

There are changes in the management of healthcare since the integration of artificial intelligence (AI) in wearable devices and remote monitoring devices. These devices are constantly collecting and analyzing biosignature information in real-time, such as blood pressure, heart rate, glucose level, and sleep cycles, due to sensor and AI. This information enables patients and health care professionals to receive relevant information on the patient's health status, as AI algorithms scan this data to identify trends, pathophysiologic changes and potential risks to the patient's health. The constant stream of personalized health information allows for the prevention and early management of chronic disease, swift intervention for new diseases, and targeted counselling on how to improve overall quality of life. Hence, the health care system is moving toward a positive, less heroic and more personal approach that empowers patients to manage their own care because of the emerging technology of wearable devices developed with the help of artificial intelligence.

1.5 Ethical Challenges and Risks of AI in Healthcare

Several ethical concerns and challenges emerge as the use of ML and AI is integrated into predictive health; to ensure that the approach is only used responsibly the following points should be addressed. Privacy is a massive issue, more so concerning the acquisition, storage, and process of health information that perhaps is very personal to the patient in question. Privacy of the patient is very important especially with the increasing use of different data in patient care with special emphasis on genomic data and EHRs. Further, there is a potential of data security risks that are likely to occur due to lack of protective cover that may result in patient's compromise. Moreover, learning algorithms can have biases that are inherent in the training data set and work to reduce the fairness in delivering Health care. Altogether, these ethical issues demonstrate the need for the development of sound ethical principles and standards that would ensure the organization of the rapidly growing sphere of predictive health care.

Figure 1.4: Ethical Challenges and considerations posed by AI implementation in Healthcare

1.5.1 Data privacy and security concerns in healthcare AI

There are huge progression in the application of artificial intelligence (AI) in the healthcare sector but it has a core issue with the data privacy and security. The large amounts of sensitive health information required for training AI-based systems are risks if adequate protection is not given to them. Following the analysis by the RUSI, which states that constant privacy impact assessments are vital when it comes to AI utilization in the national security sphere, the same is needed in healthcare. Authorizing AI systems present the potential to violate patients' rights to privacy of their information and unauthorized use of the data, thus a need for strict code of regulations on the use of AI systems. Moreover, the increase of connectivity in healthcare through the 5G technology is revolutionary for the healthcare industry, the topic again demonstrates the challenge of safe data transfer. Hence, creation of sound structures for patient protection and maintaining an ethical approach will be vital in managing the two-edged sword that AI is in healthcare settings.

1.5.2 Bias and fairness in predictive algorithms

It is quite dramatic to emphasize the necessity of fair predictive algorithms nowadays, especially when it comes to healthcare, and its outcomes for minorities. Various value biases inherent in machine learning (ML) are known to cause distortions that result in unequal patient care, thus producing low patient care outcomes. In the same studies, it is revealed that systematic bias in data and model prejudiced the algorithm and are the result of cultural and socioeconomic differences. Moreover, the systematic review questions also reveal that despite the appreciation of selection bias and implicit bias in AI studies using EHRs many of the strategies employed do not have adequate approaches for bias elimination. There is, therefore, a need to follow the principles of FAIRness from the time of data acquisition to model deployment and assessment. Therefore, eliminating these prejudices does not only benefit the moral aspect of the predictive algorithms but also guarantees healthcare solutions for all population categories.

1.5.3 Regulatory frameworks and compliance issues

Considering the use of AI ad ML in predictive health care it is crucial to set proper regulation to protect patient's interest as well as to follow ethical requirements. However, there are significant gaps with regard to these technologies in the development of regulatory frameworks that can turn these technologies into reliable methods to enhance disease diagnosis and treatment outcomes. Similarly, the current absence of standard practices for data acquisition, data preprocessing, and validation can сausеелен biases in AI systems, and, in turn, errors in diagnosis or unequal healthcare. Also, the control structures remain disparate, and the new agencies, such as the FDA, remain ill-suited to address the challenges AI in healthcare delivery presents. Previous studies have shown that these compliance matters could be well coordinated in an exclusive agency, including the mentioned "Department of Artificial Intelligence Standardization", to develop standard procedures that minimize risks and improve patients' safety and medical care (Mohammad Amini et al., 2023).

Ethical Implications

The employment of artificial intelligence in decision making concerning healthcare brings profound ethical questions with regard to autonomy of patients and consent to treatment as well as trust. The ability of AI to diagnose certain conditions and suggest treatments raises concerns over whether specific medical choices should be vested in machines. Though enhanced by AI, the medical treatment of the body requires that the patient maintain full agency over her or his decisions. Obtaining informed consent is more complicated with AI because patients must recognize that AI is part of their treatment and comprehend some of the issues and risks inherent to AI decisions. Reliability of AI applied to healthcare also depends on the openness regarding the rationale of artificial intelligence and the capacity of doctors and other healthcare workers to explain these decisions to the users. There is therefore always a delicate ethical tightrope between providing a rational justification for the use of AI in personalized medicine and preserving patient's agency, right to self-determination, and trust.

In conclusion, despite the tremendous possibilities for the growth of personalized treatment with the help of AI technologies, their integration is challenging because of numerous problems connected with bias, data protection, legislation, and, finally, questions of ethicality. As with other forms of artificial intelligence applications, the issues that have to be addressed to ensure that personalized medicine is fair and aligned to societal values require ethical consideration of the technology, innovation in the technology, reform of the regulation and of course an ongoing engagement with patients and the public.

1.6 AI's Role in Optimizing Healthcare Delivery

AI has taken its place as one of the world's most significant enabling technologies for healthcare organization and delivery on the health production functions. These facets of AI can help Healthcare systems Cut out operational wastage, likewise accelerate mundane work and also improve the care linkages. Implementation of these upgrades improves patients' treatment level and decreases costs by many folds. Another area of practical use that has been realised in administering healthcare delivery is resource management and scheduling. About patient flow managers also note that their wards experience a difficult time addressing admission, discharge, and transfers of patients in their hospitals. Based on the similar factors and patient data the tools which are backed by AI can also predict patient inflow. This capacity of forecasting helps in better distribution and management of beds, staff and medical equipments facilitating better functioning in a hospital. Likewise, the many advanced scheduling solutions that employ AI trends decide on the operational rooms, diagnostics assets, or appointments dependent on patients' preferences.

AI is also useful in removing routine office tasks so that healthcare workers can do away with some of the tasks hence allowing them to have time to attend to their patients. For instance, medical paperwork can be hastened by transcribing doctor's notes and mining unstructured data to settle on relevancy structured data with NLP. They can also also include claims processing, coding and invoicing which may cut down the time and reduce mistakes in issuing payments. AI reduces the functional barriers and increases organizational effectiveness through reduction of tasks. Another domain where AI is rather greatly evolving is in the management of the workflow. They also can track and analyse processes in a hospital in real time and notice the lack of some and possible changes for improvement. For instance, AI can identify if lab test is taking longer time or identify if there are cases where patient discharge processes are being delayed. Moreover, the advanced communication platforms like AI, backed enhance multispecialty groups interaction due to the fact that information that is sensitive and ought to be communicated from one team to another is relayed accurately and on time.

AI also assists in the supply chain where it provides forecasts on stock levels of drugs, general used products through to medical equipment. In tender supply market, forecast can be made in advance to meet the demand change early without keeping excessive stock which significantly les Kerry's cost and waste. In conclusion, the latter proves AI as very helpful in enhancing the successful and efficient functioning of the operations and workflows within the hospital facilities through the particular elements such as prediction of resource demands, as well as a range of automations. These changes do not only enhance organization productivity but also benefits patient care experiences, and create the culture of hope for much stronger and innovative healthcare delivery systems.

CHAPTER 2

AI APPLICATIONS IN CLINICAL DECISION-MAKING

2.1 Enhancing Diagnostic Accuracy Through AI

Over the last few years and particularly in the last couple of months, AI has revealed itself as an ideal tool in different markets with healthcare being the most promising one. In particular, among the subcategories of AI, deep learning, or DL has shown good applicability in increasing the diagnostic rate and improving clinical decision-making. Unlike other artificial intelligence techniques where one must handcraft features, deep learning, especially convolution neural networks (CNN) can learn features from the raw data independent of the user. These capabilities enable deep learning models to better perform in the areas that require pattern evaluation in a set of big data, so their use is critical in the medical field, especially in image-based clinical practice (Esteva et al., 2017; Z. Liu et al., 2019)the most common human malignancy, is primarily diagnosed visually, beginning with an initial clinical screening and followed potentially by dermoscopic analysis, a biopsy and histopathological examination. Automated classification of skin lesions using images is a challenging task owing to the fine-grained variability in the appearance of skin lesions. Deep convolutional neural networks (CNNs. Deep learning has the potential and has seen a vast acceptance in medical diagnostics, especially in imaging. Used in MRI, CT scans, and X-rays, radiological investigation incorporates images that are interpreted by human radiologists to spot abnormalities. However, there is a limited availability of radiologists across the world especially in LMIC countries, current and future demands turned to the necessity of developing effective AI solutions that can increase diagnostic accuracy rates and patient survival rates and reduce diagnostic errors (Rajpurkar et al., 2017)we train a 34-layer convolutional neural network which maps a sequence of ECG samples to a sequence of rhythm classes. Committees of board-certified cardiologists annotate a gold standard test set on which we compare the performance of our model to that of 6 other individual cardiologists. We exceed the average cardiologist performance in both recall (sensitivity. These existing challenges can be solved using deep learning-based diagnostic systems, which can quickly analyze medical images at a large scale and reduced cost.

It must be noted that while research in deep learning for diagnosis in healthcare has made much progress, it is not without its issues when it comes to implementation into daily practice. Incorporation of deep learning systems into healthcare requires the systems to mimic the diagnostic capabilities of human clinicians at least or better still surpass them. Also, the problem of model explanations, data protection, and the broad applicability of AI techniques to different ethnic majorities pose a persistent challenge. For example, though some deep learning-powered diagnostic tools were approved by regulatory bodies such as the FDA, independent diagnostic accuracy evaluation and meta-analysis are in their premature stages, reflecting a range of study design and reporting.

2.1.1 AI in Imaging: Revolutionizing Radiology and Pathology

Artificial Intelligence (AI) is revolutionizing the fields of radiology and pathology by providing advanced tools for enhancing diagnostic accuracy, efficiency, and workflow optimization. One of the biggest areas of machine learning, deep learning, is particularly good at detecting subtle patterns in images which include medical images like x-rays, MRI, CT scans among others. Unlike other forms of qualitative analysis, AI delivers quantitative results and that means clinicians make informed decisions. CAD for example helps the radiologists by identifying shapes such as tumors, fractures, or vascular anomalies; the work of the CAD is as efficient as those of human beings (Hosny et al., 2018). In radiology, AI supports diagnostic imaging technologies by allowing cross-consultation of information originating from a CT scan and PET scan, for example. It is especially so in early stage diagnosis where changes that can be seen may not easily be detected by human eye on the scans. For instance, early-stage lung cancer identification algorithms when applied to scans of chests has brought about signs of higher survival rates because the cancer is detected at treatable stages (Shelmerdine, 2024). In addition, AI helps to decrease diagnostic failures and inconsistent quality of services comparing to the human approach. Another area that has experienced advances through AI is pathology with a particular emphasis on digital pathology that uses algorithms to analyze high-resolution histopathological slides to identify patterns of cancer and other diseases. This in turn greatly accelerates the diagnostic process, which is especially important in those cases that cannot be addressed by the pathologists' assistant and still require the pathologist's attention. The other area of application of the AI in pathology is in diagnosis of rare diseases and treatment planning based on molecular and histological analysis of tissues.

However, there are issues with the integration of AI in radiology and pathology, including the ethical issue, data privacy, and safety and reliability standard issue. But with advancement in the research and development of AI and its integration with health care practitioners the possibilities of redefining these fields are tremendous, diagnostics take less time, more accurate and can be made available for a large number of people.

2.1.2 Detecting Rare Diseases with Advanced AI Models

Identification of rare diseases has always been a major issue in the healthcare systems and medicine in general mainly because of their low incidence, diagnostic heterogeneity and clinical heterogeneity. These advances have been more recent and have been brought about by the development of new sophisticated artificial intelligence algorithms that provide other techniques of diagnosis at an earlier stage. These models are particularly good at pattern recognition and can sift through large stores of data – EHRs, genomic data, imaging data – to try to spot signs of very rare conditions. Another category of AI is machine learning (ML), which is especially useful for searching for peculiarities in multidimensional data that usually remain undetected in the course of diagnoses based on no discrete data (Wojtara et al., 2023). Another area, which has been a joy to accomplish through the use of AI, is shortening of the diagnostic journey of rare diseases, which takes most of the years and involves a number of doctors. Deep learning is being applied in AI systems to support the integration of clinical, genetic and biochemical data which help in diagnosing conditions such as rare metabolic diseases, genetic disorders etc quickly. For example machine learning that uses genomic data to predict rare genetic mutations that may be relating to certain diseases has been very effective in helping prescribing correct treatments thereby enhancing patients' lives (Visibelli et al., 2023).

Further, AI-based techniques improve diagnostic precision due to applying NLP to derive meaningful features from textual data in clinical note and literature. This capability helps clinicians to link symptoms and laboratory findings with the diseases reported in cases and literature databases. There are also AI systems being incorporated into clinical processes; decision-support tools that can suggest the likely diagnosis based on computed patient data.

2.1.3 Integrating AI with Human Expertise for Improved Outcomes

Combining AI with human input provides some sort of double effect which greatly improves all fields that are involved with decision making. Algorithmic memory, analytical thinking, data prediction, calculation speed – all these belong to the strengths of AI, but it lacks human experience, morality, perception and innovation. This collaboration entails that the AI systems developed perform optimally, are robust and can solve real-life problems that are complicated (Johnson et al., 2022)increase revenue, and improve customer satisfaction. AI can be particularly beneficial in enhancing decision-making processes for complex and ill-structured problems that lack transparency and have unclear goals. Most AI algorithms require labeled datasets to learn the problem characteristics, draw decision boundaries, and generalize. However, most datasets collected to solve complex and ill-structured problems do not have labels. Additionally, most AI algorithms are opaque and not easily interpretable, making it hard for decision-makers to obtain model insights for developing effective solution strategies. To this end, we examine existing AI paradigms, mainly symbolic AI (SAI. One of the obvious areas of integration is in healthcare where AI models are applied in analyzing images, or patient outcome. However, all the results produced are checked by human clinicians who bring their expertise when interpreting specific findings and making decisions. Likewise, in fields of finance, and engineering, AI automates data and analytics analysis and predictive modelling and people manage strategies focusing on overall organizational goals (Khalifa & Albadawy, 2024) characterized by structured expression of ideas, data-driven arguments, and logical reasoning. However, it poses challenges such as handling vast amounts of information and complex ideas. The integration of Artificial Intelligence (AI).

One of these engagements is informed artificial intelligence (IAI), a framework of domain knowledge within the AI system. Through adaptation of human knowledge to train and improve Artificial Intelligence, the errors as well as the prejudices that come with them are minimized by IAI. For instance, AI applied in academic research incorporate human bias in labeling, data and ethic compliance, therefore amounts to relevant and meaningful results. While applying AI enable added benefits such as efficiency and scalability, human input offers a solution where outlooks including legal, moral, or ethical are beyond the AI reach, and interpretation, and flexibility in handling of emergent circumstances. Through that synergy, people and artificial intelligence are mutually building on each other's strengths to produce improved results in numerous spheres of life such as education, health, commerce, and others. AI integration thus adds efficiency to the process, as well as a responsible approach to integrating AI work on complicated problems.

2.2 Predictive AI Models for Disease Management

AI is innovative and has greatly affected the traditional medical practice introducing new techniques in disease diagnosing and treating. AI application in healthcare predictive analytics involves the use of complex formulas and machine-based learning to analyze a large amount of data in an attempt to determine the likelihood of an event that would otherwise take humans a relatively long time to deduce given similar details. Studies have revealed that these technologies increase the diagnostic accuracies and early diagnosis, help to design individual care plans, fashioning patient recovery and leading to efficient resource utilisation. The application of AI has been on the rise in the healthcare system in the recent past as enhanced data processing techniques emerged coupled with easy access to medical big data. Many AI models can integrate multiple data types including EHRs, medical images, and genomics, to get a 360-degree view of the patient.

2.2.1 Chronic Disease Management Using Predictive Tools

Self-management of chronic illnesses has become one of the significant priorities in contemporary medicine since chronic illnesses including diabetes, heart diseases, and other chronic respiratory illnesses continue to increase (Holman, 2020; Viegi et al., 2020) predictive analysis refers to a set of processes that entail analyzing prior data, statistical methods, analysis and principles of artificial intelligence to estimate the chance of occurrence of an event in the future. Advanced chronic disease management uses predictive analytics to extract the big patient data for disease prognosis, complication prediction and individualized treatment plan (Nenova & Shang, 2022)as accurate disease projections can facilitate better treatment decisions. The power of prediction is prevention, as it is easier to prevent than to reverse. In this research, we propose a data-driven model for accurate and fast disease trajectory prediction, using electronic health records (EHRs. AI improves these abilities by helping with clearer and more timely assessments, identifying hidden connections not evident to analysts, and getting better and better as it takes in more information. AI's adoption in the healthcare system has the potential of revolutionizing the control of chronic diseases, leading to enhanced early and accurate care, thus leading to reduced cost of health care.

In healthcare, I is not limited to the application of predictive analytics. It covers a broad spectrum of uses, including imaging, surgery, decision making, virtual health assistants and even the well-known concept of 'one size does not fit all' customized medicine. However, this study is on how the management of chronic diseases will be transformed by AI-Powered Predictive Analytics. Big data and machine learning algorithms enable AI systems to predict when a disease will worsen, suggest behavioral modifications to halt its progression, and advise when to seek medical attention. This proactive action improves patients' quality of care and prepares healthcare facilities for possible lowered admissions and need for extensive operations (Ngozi Samuel Uzougbo et al., 2024).

However, there are significant ethical and regulatory obstacles to overcome before the benefits of using AI to manage chronic diseases can be fully realized. Since AI in healthcare is still in its infancy, there are several concerns about data security and privacy as well as adherence to current regulations. This study therefore suggests that there is need to develop sound regulations which can address the safety and efficiently of AI systems as well as promoting equity in the market. Furthermore, ethical concerns include those pertaining to patient privacy, prejudice in AI, openness in AI decision-making, and informed permission for AI use in healthcare.

2.2.2 AI's Role in Preventing Cardiovascular and Metabolic Disorders

Since artificial intelligence (AI) provides sophisticated diagnostic and risk assessment tools, it has emerged as a potent solution for the management and prediction of metabolic and cardiovascular diseases. These conditions, which rank among the leading causes of morbidity and death worldwide, are typically brought on by a variety of factors, such as lifestyle choices, genetic predisposition, the ecology of illnesses, and others. AI systems present a significant advantage in the present healthcare system owing to their capability to analyze large datasets and search for subtle patterns.

The AI technology has particularly hailed in flagging people who are at risk of developing cardiovascular diseases (CVDs). For instance, machine learning models diagnose given patient data, including past medical history, DNA, and lifestyle to determine likelihood of hypertension, diabetes, and heart failure. This makes it possible for the healthcare providers to act proactively, for instance the doctor may opt for the patient to change their lifestyle or start with treatment right away (Dalakoti et al., 2024). Besides, AI improves diagnosis due to the integration of information from imaging techniques, for instance, echocardiography, computed tomography and wearable technology that depicts real time vital signs including heartbeat and glucose levels. Continuous monitoring underpinned by AI informs patients and clinicians of abnormalities but also gives them the tools to stop the progression of the disease. In diseases such as diabetes, AI algorithms estimate the fluctuations of glucose levels and adjust the amount of insulin needed, with great effectiveness. Besides personal impacts, AI helps public health initiatives find risk patterns in populations. In this way, the epidemiological data can help policymakers to conceptualize the specific prevention strategies, including the community programmed towards obesity and smoking cessation. Further, the combination of AI with IoT devices has provided the opportunity to develop smart health ecosystem that provides extended and preventive health care (Olawade et al., 2024). AI's role in influencing the cardiovascular and metabolic disorders perception has to do with its ability to bring precision medicine together with prevention approaches. In this way, with the help of AI, patient's condition can be optimized and the disease prevalence may be minimized in the case of high-risk patients.

2.3 Personalization in Medicine Through AI

Drugs that work for some people but not for others, or that cause negative effects in others, are always unexpected problems. There is also the issue of why some people get certain diseases, like cancer, while others do not. Age and lifestyle, as well as genetic makeup, may be contributing factors to these issues. believes that each patient's condition should be treated as distinct by medicine, using medicines based on the patient's biology and medical history. Precision or personalized medicine is the term used to describe this method of practicing medicine.

In order to obtain effective treatment, patients with identical diagnostic results should not be treated in the same manner; instead, they can undergo various treatments. As a subfield or extension of the medical sciences, personalized medicine uses clinical judgement and practice to provide patients with individualized healthcare. According to the theory, the main goals of personalized medicine are to accurately diagnose patients, maximize the best possible treatment, and forecast a person's likelihood of contracting an illness.

This is made possible by genetic data, which is included into baseline data for the purpose of customizing or adjusting medical administration or therapy. Although few common genetic variants have contributed to our understanding, most reproducible findings do not identify common genes that underlie susceptibility or protection from disease. Instead, our present understanding focusses mostly on uncommon genetic variants. The field of medicine has expanded dramatically over the years, and a lot of attention has been paid to the possibility of preventing diseases by using contemporary technologies to determine a person's risk of contracting an illness and to provide treatments (perhaps medication) to prevent the disease from developing. In addition, clinical staff—such as physicians and pharmacists—can provide healthcare services considerably more efficiently by using technology than they could using conventional methods.

In order to improve the precision and accuracy of disease detection, treatment, and medication delivery, artificial intelligence approaches are crucial for establishing or developing personalized medicine. Controlling unfavorable drug reactions and enzyme metabolism causes some people to have trouble getting rid of medications from their bodies, which can lead to overdose, while others get rid of the drug before it has a chance to accomplish its job. These days, electronic health record (EHR) systems and the use of computers in hospitals and clinics to document medical activities give medical knowledge and data that may be used as a standard to improve the delivery of medical services.

2.3.1 Role of AI in Tailoring Drug Therapies

One of the keys to the notion of personalized medicine is the fact that AI is gradually revolutionizing the sphere of medicine as a whole by making it possible to deliver customized drug therapies for every patient. AI uses big data, including genomic data, medical histories, and real-time health data, to determine the most effective treatment plans. Thus, this approach not only increases the effectiveness of the existing pharmacological preparations but also reduces the chances of possible side effects making treatment outcomes safer and more effective. This is probably the most obvious way through which AI advances individualized drug treatments because it uses statistical models. Personalized data including genetic markers and metabolic profiles of patients are used by machine learning algorithms to understand, how such patients will react to certain medications. For example, pharmacogenomics which is defined as the study of how genetic variation influences drug response fully benefits from AI. machines can predict which of the genetic markers impact drug metabolism so that physicians can give patients the right amounts of medicine or recommend other drugs they are more compatible with (Ejike Innocent Nwankwo et al., 2024)promising a new era of precision healthcare. This paper explores the role of AI in revolutionizing drug therapies by tailoring treatments to individual patient profiles, thereby optimizing therapeutic outcomes and minimizing risks. AI leverages vast amounts of medical data, including genetic information, electronic health records (EHRs.

AI also accelerates drug discovery and development, a traditionally lengthy and expensive process. By simulating biological processes and analyzing clinical trial data, AI identifies potential drug candidates and predicts their efficacy in specific patient populations. This not only reduces costs but also ensures that newly developed drugs are more compatible with individual patient profiles. Moreover, AI-powered systems enhance real-time decision-making in clinical settings. For example, in oncology, AI integrates data from wearable devices, imaging, and laboratory results to continuously monitor patient responses to treatment. This dynamic feedback enables timely adjustments to drug regimens, ensuring that therapy remains effective throughout the course of treatment (Taherdoost & Ghofrani, 2024).

Incorporation of AI in bespoke medicine also solves issues concerning polypharmacy, which is common with chronic diseases. With the help of the assessment of the interactions and folds combining effects AI systems offer optimized and safer medication regimens geared towards the patient's needs. Further, the advancement of delivery systems by the use AI and especially nanotechnology in delivering precision therapies to the requisite tissues reinforces the capability of delivering medication. Taken collectively, the application of AI to drug therapy personalization can be described as a revolution in medicine that has the potential for bringing about actual improvements in patient results and cost savings due to the previously unimaginable level of individualized treatment.

2.3.2 Advances in Genomic Sequencing and Personalized Care

The development of genomic sequencing in medicine has greatly helped the custom approach to patient treatment by allowing for individualized medical treatment. Now widely known as next-generation sequencing (NGS), the technologies differ from Sanger method in that they are faster and more accurate and have recently offered the ability to decode human genomes at a fraction of the cost and time it took previously. Such innovations have offered important kinds of information regarding genetic changes that lead to diseases and thus set the stage for a personalized approach to disease treatment. The Human Genome Project was finalised in the year 2003 through which the whole of the human genome was sequenced which provided a platform for subsequent analysis (Wilson & Nicholls, 2015). Personalized care uses patients' genomic information to guide the kind of treatment the patient needs. For instance, pharmacogenomics applies genetic information for the purpose of identifying how the patient will be affected by a particular drug or how effective the drug will be to the patient. Sequencing technology has also improved the discovery of biomarkers, critical for diagnosing the likes of cancer or particular inherited diseases. These biomarkers facilitate the creation of targeted therapies, composites that are established to make contact with the molecular attributes of a patient's disease state, according to Ginsburg and Willard in Genomic and Personalized Medicine. In addition, the genomic sequencing has shifted prenatal testing into the realm of non-invasive prenatal testing (NIPT) that has an extraordinary accuracy when it comes to diagnosing fetal genetic disorders. The combination of genomic data with artificial intelligence has also helped to standardize the assessment of risk for hard-to-diagnose diseases such as diabetes as well as heart diseases. These systems can be very useful in predicting disease risks as well as tackling ways of preventing them when large amounts of data are involved (Prins et al., 2021)

The most far-reaching consequence of genomic sequencing is the ability to make genomic equity a reality that will foster good health. Scholars are developing the algorithms and tools to make sure that people with color receive the benefits from the genomic data, as for a long, genetic research are skewed in any positive way. Due to its advances and improvements, sequencing stands to revolutionalise health care through early detection, tailored interventions and risk-reduction. Therefore, through the improved genomic sequencing it has been apparent that personalized medicine is already revolutionizing the provision of patient care through more efficient, individualized and fair means.

2.4 Smart Healthcare, IoT, and Machine Learning: A Complete Survey

In our daily lives, healthcare is essential. With the right care, health conditions can be diagonalised and avoided in their early stages. With the use of various curing equipment, like as CT, MRI, PET, etc., it is simple to identify any abnormalities that are present inside our bodies or beneath the skin. Additionally, some rare illnesses, such as heart attacks and strokes, are easily preventable in their early stages. Modern health care systems are struggling due to the unforeseen spread of degenerative diseases in large numbers brought on by the world's population growth, and there is an extremely high need for funds for everything from hospital beds to physicians and nurses. The strain on healthcare systems must be lessened in order to preserve the level of quality and grade of care that is offered at its best. One possible way to lessen the strain on healthcare systems is through the Internet of Things (IoT). Previously, the incidental examination of diabetic patients was detailed, and individuals with specific infections, like Parkinson's disease, were also observed. Numerous rehabilitation techniques, such as assisting rehabilitation, are used in order to continuously monitor the patients' development, as researchers seek to fulfil specific reasons for curing diseases at an early stage. Given the vast amount of data that exists today, care should be given to data preparation, storage, and analysis, with little emphasis on incorporating those into a system and making use of them. To provide reliable distant information transfer, a variety of wearable frameworks are suggested. IT and medical clinic administrators are both fussing over IoT devices and information security. One area of study that may be a subset of artificial intelligence (AI) is artificial reasoning. By using human logic, we will create a better and more prosperous future. Without being specifically changed, AI may be able to learn from references and facts. The data is supported by the traditional computation, and reasoning is provided based on the data, rather than writing code. Web design, spam filtering, ad placement, stock trading, and other areas are heavily reliant on AI. Even if it is anticipated that obtaining access to this wealth of knowledge will result in major advancements in research and design as well as improvements to the natural world, it also brings about enormous experiences at the same time. According to a McKinsey Global Institute assessment, artificial intelligence (AI) will be the primary force behind the massive development of the Internet of Things (IoT), which envisions the ability to collaborate remotely and verify the accuracy of articles (items) via the Internet. Science and information reliant on wireless sensing hub technology are now discussed in the health care environment. Due to the specific explanation of heart problems and assault, which is a direct result of the lack of enough therapeutic upkeep for patients at the necessary moment, patients are facing an uncertain situation of prevision end. This will allow for the unique identification of elderly patients, children, and enlightening professionals, friends, and family. Therefore, we are considering a creative project to use Patient Health Monitoring, which makes use of sensor innovation and the internet to notify friends and family in the event of problems, to create such surprise passing rates. Additionally, we have seen ML processes being used to continuous enhancements in several Internet of Things (IoT) domains.

2.4.1 Overview of IoT in Smart Healthcare Systems

The phrase "Internet of Things" (IoT) encompasses a wide range of applications, standards, technologies, and initiatives. Fundamentally, it is an Internet-connected network of objects. These include IoT devices and physical IoT-enabled objects. The foundation and core of what the Internet of Things (IoT) represents and enables are things and data. IoT assets and devices are outfitted with software and electronic parts to collect, organize, and distribute data.

The phrase "Internet of Things" was coined by Kevin Ashton. In the late 1990s, he researched radio frequency identification (RFID), a technique that enables tiny radio frequency tags with information that can be read from a distance to be attached to different subjects. In a plastic case, it functions as a tiny sticker or unique label that, for instance, makes it possible to follow the flow of goods, enhancing the supply management system and maybe preventing theft. In the trade sector, these RFID tags are now frequently used. Additionally, the term "Internet of Things" was coined by Kevin Ashton to describe the fundamental concept of his innovation. He once proposed that every single item in the Internet of Things would have a digital equivalent that would serve as its virtual image.

One of the most noble applications of IoT is in healthcare. Doctors can use IoT to provide online assistance to patients. Doctor-patient distance can be greatly decreased using portable IoT-based health monitoring devices. IoT enables you to treat each patient as an individual, assess their current state of health, and determine the best course of action for them. With portable sensors, physicians may keep an eye on their patients' health from a distance and react instantly. But real-time measures need a constant

Internet connection. Despite its rapid development, IoT in healthcare is still not fully utilized in various medical sectors (Sadoughi et al., 2020)including nursing, rehabilitation sciences, ambient assisted living (AAL. There are still certain challenges in creating suitable Internet applications for traditional medicine. The IoT is likely to draw more medical researchers in the upcoming years, as the quantity of these studies has significantly increased.

In order for modern medical practitioners to make well-informed and individualized judgements, they must gather a significant amount of big data and analyses and understand it. All of it requires a lot of time and work. This procedure can be sped up and made easier by new IoT technology. There is an increasing volume of digital medical data in relation to the widespread adoption of electronic health registration. It takes time to view and evaluate all of this information in its entirety. Additionally, it is necessary to train medical personnel on AI-based technology that is closely related to the Internet of Things.

By using digital technologies like AI and the Internet of Things in concert, doctors may better customize patient care. In order to closely monitor the development of a certain disease or process, these technologies can manage a far larger number of data for storage and analysis. Positive advances in healthcare management can be achieved by skillfully fusing the potential of new techniques for diagnosis, collection, and analysis with real-world personal experience.

Network-enabled technologies, which include wearable and portable gadgets that may trigger, detect, synergies, and link with other similar media over the Internet, are eventually introduced by the Internet of Things. Data production, consumption, and distribution are being profoundly altered by the Internet of Things. In contrast to IoT technologies, which periodically collect and process ecological data that impacts an individual's health, average individuals regularly utilize these systems to track their food consumption, sleep, vital signs, exercise, and other physical states. In the end, this interoperability has sparked the development of innovative medicinal substitutes.

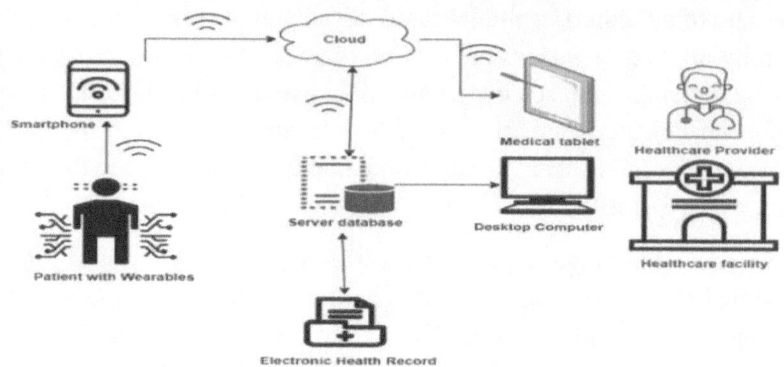

Figure 2.1:   The concept of IoT in healthcare

Source: - (Paranjape et al., 2020)

2.4.2 Machine Learning for Real-Time Health Monitoring

Nowadays, real-time health monitoring is regarded as one of the most advantageous aspects of machine learning (ML), which offers the capacity to quickly and accurately analyse vast amounts of data. It is possible to study and deliver actionable insights in real time from real-time data monitoring from IoMT sensors and health monitoring wearables by using algorithms that analyse trends and make predictions. In tracking conditions like diabetes and hypertension, where information gathered can be used to provide recommendations for illness monitoring, this feature is particularly crucial. Of the many uses of ML in real-time health monitoring, one of the most relevant is anomaly detection. Higher-level paradigms, including deep machine learning patterns and integrative formulations incorporating CNNs integrated with MLPs, are employed to detect anomalies in the physiological data, including heart rates or oxygen levels (Nizamuddin et al., 2024)particularly in real-time health monitoring and predictive interventions for chronic diseases, has many benefits but also many drawbacks. Existing health risk prediction algorithms face accuracy issues and, due to the wide variety of health profiles, general algorithm applicability is problematic. The proposed model solves this issue by using an advanced AI framework to improve the accuracy of the prediction of Chronic Kidney Disease (CKD. These systems help to predict development of some clinical states, for example, cardiac arrhythmias or respiratory distress, thus equipping the caregivers for an appropriate reaction.

Another significant application is the control of human health, specifically according to each person's unique traits. As the patient's data changes over time, the algorithm's predictions and suggestions will be tailored to the patient because machine learning algorithms are able to adjust to the patient. Such customisation improves the monitoring system's overall effectiveness and lowers the frequency of false alarms. Real time health monitoring has been improved through the application of ML in conjunction with cloud computing and Internet of Medical Things (IoMT) devices. Data records are processed in real-time, thus ensuring that information can be aggregated and converted to dashboards that clinicians can use to monitor a patient's health status remotely. Such advancements have been very useful in RPM systems especially during the Covid – 19 outbreak whereby physical access to hospitals was limited. However, there are some limitations and threats when using ML in health monitoring such as; Data privacy; quality data; and algorithmic bias. These problems are why ethical principles and proper validation of the model before it can be released into the wild are crucial (Janani et al., 2023).

2.5 AI in Intensive and Emergency Care

Any time a patient experiences an emergency, calling the emergency services is the first step in that patient's medical care plan. Before transferring the case to EMS, an emergency dispatcher is expected to receive triage information, evaluate the situation based on its severity, deploy response resources, and provide verbal instructions. Therefore, the timely and accurate assessment is especially important in this case, and it is even more necessary in some particular situation when it can be hard to determine the triage, for example, in case of a large-scale disaster or pandemic. However, in this domain, AI is relatively limited, and there are only a few cases in which AI offers the chance to manage assessment and decision-making at a higher level.

For instance, commercial (although investigational) systems can be used as the second listener during the call using ASR. Intended to be able to filter pertinent data in real time, these systems are also designed to identify symptoms that are indicative of such critical conditions and indicate possible secondary questions which will not be asked otherwise. It then automatically produces comprehensive case notes thus minimizing on the administrative work involved.

A retrospective trial has been conducted to evaluate the underlying technology (Byrsell et al., 2021), which evaluated the artificial intelligence-driven ASR system's recognition time for out-of-hospital cardiac arrest (OHCA), finding that the AI outperformed the dispatcher (median time to recognition 72 vs. 94 s). In Denmark, a randomized clinical trial evaluated a comparable system. (Blomberg et al., 2021)resulting in lost opportunities to save lives by initiating cardiopulmonary resuscitation. Objective: To examine how a machine learning model trained to identify OHCA and alert dispatchers during emergency calls affected OHCA recognition and response. Design, Setting, and Participants: This double-masked, 2-group, randomized clinical trial analyzed all calls to emergency number 112 (equivalent to 911, which looked at how often dispatchers recognised OHCA. The employed ASR model alerted the dispatcher by listening for indicators that might point to OHCA. The machine learning model exhibited a lower positive predictive value (17.8 vs. 97.4%), although surpassing dispatcher identification rates of OHCA (85.0 vs. 77.5%). Notifying the dispatcher did not result in noticeably higher recognition rates (93.1% in the intervention group vs. 90.5% in the control group) for calls that the machine learning model suspected of being OHCA. Although these findings show that these technologies require further development before they can consistently support human judgement, they do show significant advancements through the use of innovative methods.

2.5.1 Real-Time Monitoring in Intensive Care Units (ICUs)

Numerous data points are often gathered for patients admitted to the intensive care unit. Hence, it is especially well-suited for the use of machine learning models that aid physicians in medical diagnosis, treatment, and decision-making. The growing body of work in this area reflects the applicability of machine learning for the intensive care unit. Several recent initiatives to open up ICU research resources to academics are the main drivers of this upsurge. Notable databases include the Netherlands' AmsterdamUMCdb and the United States' eICU and Medical Information Mart for Intensive Care (MIMIC) databases (Thoral, Peppink, et al., 2021). Researchers investigating the potential and prediction skills of machine learning were made possible by these databases.

Early warning systems, prognostic tools, treatment-suggestive models, disease phenotyping, and resource management are the general categories into which use cases in the intensive care unit can be divided. A systematic review conducted in 2021 (van de Sande et al., 2021)and to improve quality and efficiency of care, there is a need for adequate and efficient clinical decision-making. The advancement of artificial intelligence (AI reveals that the majority of artificial intelligence research in the intensive care unit is done to forecast complications (22.2%), then mortality (20.6%), prognostic model improvement (18.4%), and subpopulation classification (11.7%). Physiological threshold determination (4.9%), length of stay prediction (4.4%), and alert reduction (4.3%) are other situations that have been explored. Just 18 of the 494 papers that made up this systematic review were prospectively examined. In 2020, just 1% of ICU machine learning models were ready for real-time testing (phase 6), while 93% were in the model prototype and development phase (phases 3–4) (Fleuren et al., 2020).

A severe sepsis prediction algorithm was evaluated in a single-center randomised clinical trial, making it one of the few machine learning models for critical care medicine that has been validated in practice. The experimental group experienced a substantial decrease in in-hospital mortality (8.96 vs. 21.3%; P¼ 0.018) and average hospital length of stay (13.0 vs. 10.3 days; P¼ 0.042) [19]. Nonetheless, it is generally anticipated that in the near future, additional models will be placed at the bedsides of patients in critical condition An exploratory model that predicts which patients can be safely discharged from intensive care is a potential example (Thoral, Fornasa, et al., 2021), It has recently been demonstrated to maintain performance after retraining and external assessment.

Studies that use a machine learning technique called reinforcement learning in the intensive care unit are particularly intriguing. Reinforcement learning is concerned with automatically performing or recommending learnt best behaviours in a dynamic environment in order to maximize a particular outcome. To be more precise, these algorithms can offer sequential recommendations for ICU therapy, such as the best ratio of fluids to vasopressors or ventilator settings. There are no published articles that examine performance in a prospective scenario, as far as the authors are aware, however the use of reinforcement learning algorithms in retrospective databases shows promise (Otten et al., 2024)

2.5.2 Predicting Patient Outcomes in Critical Care Settings

Assessing the outcomes in the critical care delivery system is one of the most significant aspects of the current role of the healthcare industry. In diverse ICUs with patients, who have a high chance of clinical worsening, risk assessments of patients' outcomes, including survival, improvement or deterioration, are crucial for preventing adverse events. A number of ML models have been utilized more and more commonly in this field due to application based on large amount of patient data to discover patterns and possible futures.

The most widely applied means of capturing patient outcomes are the predictive algorithms, which take into account patient data acquired from various sources including EHR, biomedical measurements, and tests. These systems use statistical and machine learning algorithms, decision tree, neural network, support vector machine to process real-time data and generate probability of event like organ failure, sepsis, mortality etc. For instance, models created from a big data source of ICU patients can estimate the risk factors by factors such as blood pressure, pulse rate, oxygen level, and biomarkers and make predictions of the possibility of complications or survival rates (Janani et al., 2023).

Another important area where ML helps in outcome prediction is in handling of sepsis which is a deadly disease that needs attention. The use of ML algorithms can make a diagnosis of sepsis at an early stage by being able to detect changes in vital signs and laboratory tests before they become noticeable clinically. Such predictive models can help the healthcare provider to start immediate treatment, which can be lifesaving. Likewise, there are quantitative models to forecast the length of ICU stay, the likelihood of requiring mechanical ventilation, and prognosis in improving care plan and discharging patients more appropriately. However, with predictive modelling there comes several issues. A limitation of this study is the selection bias of the models as a result of the quality and type of data used in the analysis. However, the implementation of these models into clinical practice has constraints like clinician's trust on AI systems, data confidentiality and the ability of the systems to process data in real time. Nonetheless, all stated challenges can be managed to support the increasingly beneficial role that predictive analytics has in strengthening the clinical decision-making in critical care.

2.5.3 Enhancing Emergency Response Through AI Tools

Everyone knows about the importance of the emergency services to save people's lives and it is possible to note that the services offered on the market are experiencing some challenges that can impact on the service delivery. This is why the lack of new information to the medical record of a sick person is one of these difficulties. The ambulance's lack of the history of an unwell person may cause harm to the life of the sick individual and consume time in addressing the situation in the medical facility. The pre-hospital time spent can be very important for the benefits or drawbacks of the sick patient, and this pre-hospital time is closely related to this problem. The impacts of ambulance time and transportation are definitively assessed and well-known. The patient's emergency medical state and illness are extremely vital issues, and the lack of information about them can definitely have a negative impact on the patient's outcomes. Unfortunately, the absence of certain preexisting information for the relevant patient is unavoidable for the ambulance staff (Bates et al., 2023). The vital information and documents for sick individuals are crucial. Public health protection services must have the necessary IT infrastructure and mechanisms in place. Data flows and communication between units are essential, especially during emergencies. Data exchange occurs automatically between emergency service vehicles and hospitals via a middleware system. The ambulance service utilizes these middleware components, making each ambulance an always-online mobile workstation connected to the central medical record system. During preprocessing, demand and traffic classification are managed by the radio resource control interface. Subsequently, the call is transmitted to the emergency radio, enabling the driver console to control the call and access content and source information (A. Torad & H. Hossamel-din, 2021)

Emergency Response The primary concern during an emergency is to ensure the victim reaches the hospital in the shortest time possible. With a GPS receiver and assisted software, dispatchers can view the location of all available units and assign tasks to the nearest available unit. Path guidance software, taking current traffic conditions into account, is used by the driver of an ambulance to reach the destination as soon as possible. In large and busy cities, path guidance software plays a significant role in reducing travel time. With a single control center, cities can manage emergency vehicles to a fleet capacity of dozens or a few hundred; coordination is relatively simple. However, coordination becomes much more complicated when managing private vehicles at the individual level. Ultimately, hopes to turn all car radios into small twoway radios that instantly turn each vehicle into its hero associated with managing the traffic. Coverage becomes complete and continuous because a relatively large number of registered commuters are willing to assist. As an alternative solution, services could be coupled with path guidance and a refund program to enlist private individuals under most circumstances to promote a high degree of participation (X. Chen et al., 2021).

Diagnosis and Health Care In the case of remote areas, it takes hours or even days for a patient to reach a hospital in the city. To address these issues, through tele diagnosis, it is possible to connect on-site medical staff with city hospitals, signifying that medical separation can be monitored from far away. Nowadays, miniature drones that can fly quickly and do not have communication problems are available. Hospitals can predict the distribution of patients by understanding their individual medical histories. To balance the load of each hospital, patients can be redirected to the most appropriate hospital. can play a pivotal role in ensuring patients can be returned to a hospital as quickly as possible (de Araújo Novaes, 2019).

Health and Stress Monitoring In step with the 'Internet of Things,' people can be continuously monitored, and their health can be observed by shifts in behavior. Many public service announcements are designed to detect, for example, falling and relocation patterns of seniors. Furthermore, the degree of stress-related physiological reactions and behavior can be learned by continually monitoring emergency medical staff. By issuing a warning to the driver, the software can also record emergency vehicle drivers who exhibit symptoms of fatigue. By analyzing the data, paths with a high correlation with negative emotions can be identified. In addition to trying to improve the paths both physically and emotionally, manufacturers can also upgrade the ambulance for journeys that are likely to be lengthy by creating specific comfort specifications. By managing healthcare teams, hospital stress can also be recognized and filtered (Javaid et al., 2021).

2.6 Improving Medical Imaging with AI

The convergence of artificial intelligence (AI) and medical imaging stands as one of the most promising frontiers in modern healthcare. As biomedical imaging data proliferate and the complexities of image interpretation grow, the demand for tools that can augment the interpretation and analysis of this data has never been greater. The size, skill set, or time constraints of the human workforce cannot keep pace with the burgeoning amount of medical data. Herein lies the compelling promise of AI: the ability to train machines to possess human-like abilities and deliver high-quality outcomes independently of a person's size, skill set, or time constraints. Intelligent systems can be trained to learn the complex mapping from the acquired data to its interpretations fully autonomously, rapidly, reproducibly, and at large scales. While the early success of AI in radiology was predicated on the automatic detection of findings in images, its subsequent proliferation across many imaging modalities and aspects has broadened its influence in the field of medical imaging. AI began with the detection of known phenomena in medical images. Since the early 1990s, a wide variety of sophisticated, innovative, and clinically impactful detection systems have been described, some resulting in commercial products. With the advent of deep learning and the availability of large annotated datasets, the detection of unseen phenomena fully autonomously in images delineating, counting, and characterizing a multitude of findings in different modalities has been revolutionized. Detection systems for COVID-19 and other viral infections in chest X-rays and CT scans have become invaluable during public health crises, while the detection of more routine findings, such as tumors in pathology, has transformed workflows and dramatically improved patient care (Castiglioni et al., 2021). Robustly detecting a known finding across a wide range of images with variance in contrast, field of view (FOV), acquisition parameters, and more is among the most widely acknowledged challenges in medical imaging. Though diverse, medical imaging data share several key aspects that can facilitate this endeavor. Importantly, diseases occur spatially and temporally within the anatomy; the physiology pathologically drives these phenomena, and both types of human knowledge are encoded in relatively simple differential equations governing three-dimensional (3D) and temporal processes. Bridging this knowledge gap between the two domains heralds a new golden age of biomedical imaging (Y. Liu & Yeoh, 2021)

2.6.1 Role of AI in Automated Image Analysis

Artificial intelligence (AI) techniques hold significant promise in enhancing the performance of medical imaging systems. Such techniques can potentially improve and speed up both the interpretation of medical images and the reconstruction and enhancement of the images themselves. AI has found widespread applications in the field of medical imaging, particularly in the two primary areas of diagnosis and disease detection as well as image reconstruction and enhancement (Gichoya et al., 2022)yet there is no known correlation for race on medical imaging that would be obvious to human experts when interpreting the images. We aimed to conduct a comprehensive evaluation of the ability of AI to recognise a patient's racial identity from medical images. Methods: Using private (Emory CXR, Emory Chest CT, Emory Cervical Spine, and Emory Mammogram. Beside, AI has developed in the medical sector, especially in the diagnosis of diseases. It can diagnose various imaging studies and can detect diseases such as Crohn's Disease, Alzheimer's Disease, Pulmonary Embolism, Cardiovascular Diseases, Kidney Stones, and Cancer. AI's machine learning can analyze great quantities of imaging data and distinguish pathologies and correlations with diseases. This leads to early diagnosis as well as better results for the patients. AI also increases the resolution of images making it easier to diagnose diseases as compared to the image without AI superimposition. It can include individualized treatment recommendations and track the course of severe illnesses and the efficacy of treatment. Disease detection, diagnosis and treatment has been revolutionized by AI and has the capacity to revolutionize health care globally (Willemink et al., 2020)

AI is proving to be on the rise in different fields especially in the health sectors as mentioned above. At the present, the healthcare industry is bearing the brunt of AI to enhance the quality of living human beings and also in the identification of diseases that are in the initial stage, which is beneficent for health. Medical imaging is still very crucial in the health sector since it offers the correct view on the body interior. Right now there has been advancement in Medical Imaging whereby AI is used in the processes and helps Radiologist in diagnosis. Automated foreign object detection is performed with the help of computer vision. Automated fracture detection and classification using deep learning techniques on X-ray images are also being researched. Automated tumor detection in CT and MRI images of the brain is also a hot topic of research with the application of deep learning techniques. Other research trends also include sorting of CT scan images, chest X-ray based classification of COVID-19, and so on. Medical imaging is the technique of understanding the medical condition of the body with the help of images. Imaging is basically a photograph of any object captured in a particular frequency band. In the case of medical imaging, the situation is similar, but here the object is the human body. Different imaging techniques use different aspects of the human body to generate the image. Different imaging techniques are used to capture the images in different frequency bands of energy. The images captured in the visual frequency range are called optical imaging. Similarly, enthusiasm within the electromagnetic range yields pictures called microwave imaging, infrared imaging, etc. Other than these imaging approaches, numerous other techniques like sound imaging, i.e., ultrasound; magnetic imaging, i.e., MRI; penetration into the body imaging, i.e., X-ray; etc., are utilized, each with its peculiar qualities. These techniques have unique properties of penetrating the body according to their frequency bands, which assist in image formation (Tadiboina, 2022).

2.6.2 Advancements in CT Scans, MRI, and Ultrasound Technologies

In order to diagnose and cure a variety of illnesses, imaging is quite important. Physical signals are used by a variety of imaging technologies, such as Positron Emission Tomography (PET), Computed Tomography (CT), Magnetic Resonance Imaging (MRI), and optical imaging, to create images of tissues.

However, the efficacy of these imaging techniques can be significantly enhanced with the integration of deep learning methodologies, rendering it a ubiquitous framework for image reconstruction and enhancement in computed imaging. The use of preprocessing techniques can significantly enhance the quality of scanned medical pictures by utilising deep learning algorithms. More precise diagnosis and more efficient therapies are now possible thanks to the developments in this field, which have produced a number of deep learning-enhanced methods specifically made to improve simulated medical images (Avanzo et al., 2020). Currently, deep learning is applied to image artifact elimination, including magnetic resonance imaging denoising, computer tomography metal artifact attenuation, and optical coherence tomography speckle reduction. These solutions comprise data-based and model-based approaches, using deep learning as both prior and posterior. Future development in the hardware will improve the aspects of the computational speed along with the implementation of algorithms. Joint reconstruction and sparse image recovery from encoded projections have become topical leading to a fusion of coding strategies and reconstruction methods. In this case, convolutional neural networks are used as end to end post processing operators used to learn the inverse of an encoder function. All in all, there is a wide application of machine learning based image reconstruction in different imaging modalities as deep learning methods are general (Y. Wang et al., 2021).

2.6.3 Reducing Diagnostic Errors Using Machine Learning Models

Diagnostic mistakes are an important problem in healthcare, and machine learning (ML) models are now being applied to eliminate such errors. The use of big data to inform clinical practice can improve diagnosis because ML algorithms do not commit human errors when analyzing large data samples. These models analyze data coming from Electronic Health Records, laboratory findings, images, etc. and find patterns that may not be easy for a clinician to detect. There is also a vast use of the application of ML in the diagnosis of diagnostic mistakes such as HIT, which are dangerous to the patient if a doctor misdiagnoses them. Modern scholars have designed ML models that estimate the risk of HIT where misdiagnosis has been minimized across the healthcare industry (Nilius et al., 2023). Apart from increasing the efficacy of diagnoses, several applications of ML models can minimize sources of variability that are characteristic of human practitioners, for instance, inbuilt bias or burnout. For example, electronic triggering in the EHR systems can identify possible diagnostic errors and give the clinician an opportunity to validate diagnosis before the final decision (Zimolzak et al., 2024). These automated systems guarantee that conditions, including sepsis or cancer, are diagnosed early, and are less likely to be missed to facilitate early intervention. Finally, it can be stated that the adoption of ML in healthcare systems has potential to increase diagnostic accuracy and to decrease the danger of bringing about negative medical consequences for the individual patient.

2.7 Artificial Intelligence in Biometric: Uncovering Intricacies of Human Body and Mind

Despite having many physical traits in common, humans are not exact duplicates of one another. Despite their individuality, they can be compared because of shared characteristics. One of the most basic ways that people have bonded with one another as unique individuals is through facial recognition. In actuality, human visual information processing includes the ability to recognise someone. Long before there were mirrors in the ancient world (the Greeks employed hand mirrors for grooming about the fifth century BCE), people's descriptions of their faces were always based on how someone else looked at them or, at most, how they described their own reflection in clear, sunlight-lit water. For example, some people were given nicknames because of distinguishing characteristics on their forehead, nose, eyes, eyebrows, ears, and cheeks, or because of obvious markings like freckles or birthmarks. All of these were common methods of remembering people, not for discriminatory reasons but just for identification. It was feasible to know and recall everyone in villages with less than 250 families (Author, 2011), especially given that relations possessed similar and familial features.

These unique bodily traits are now referred to as biometrics. Since the turn of the century, we have utilized biometrics, like fingerprints, to indicate individuality (e.g., Scotland Yard introduced the Galton–Henry system of fingerprint classification released in June 1900). Automated fingerprint matching was in place by the middle of the 1980s in the United States, and by the 1990s, 500 automatic fingerprint identification systems (AFIS) were being used to convict criminals (Rao et al., 2023). Automation was employed for the first time to cross-check details with the installation of AFIS. High-resolution cameras have replaced old ink-based technologies to collect millions of minutiae globally (for example, India's Aadhaar, the world's largest biometric ID system, has systematically collected over a billion fingerprints). 220,000 fingerprint records from over 17,000 crime scene markings are available in Interpol's AFIS alone, which does 3000 comparisons daily. As a result, automated facial recognition has only been feasible and widely used in the past 20 years for a wide range of purposes, including tracking employee and student attendance, reducing retail crime, unlocking phones, and finding missing people.

2.7.1 Understanding Biometrics: Physical and Behavioral Attributes

Biometrics, a field that focuses on the measurement and statistical analysis of human physiological and behavioral characteristics, has emerged as a cornerstone in modern healthcare and security systems. Among the main types of physiological characteristics one can identify fingerprints, facial structures, iris and voice recognition as the most reliable and constant signs for authentication. Behavioral attributes on the other hand includes typing rhythm gait and speech that gives an extra angle of how an individual executes certain tasks, this may be plagued with health conditions or emotional instabilities (Maltoni et al., 2017). In the context of healthcare, biometric is used more actively in diagnostics and treatment of diseases, inpatient observation, and individual approach. For instance, voice biomarkers are associated with respiratory and neurological diseases; gait analysis can identify initial signs of musculoskeletal/ neurological diseases such as Parkinson's Disease. Likewise, biometric systems integrated with AI can detect small changes to the face that signal stress, fatigue or development of certain diseases and this can be used in early diagnosis.

It is however important to note that biometrics in healthcare is not only in the diagnostic applications of physical and behavioural biometrics. These attributes are being utilized to improve the patient safety, control of adherence to the prescribed treatment, and secure access to patients' records. Biometrics systems when combined with AI improve the efficiency and accuracy of these applications, due to the real-time analysis of data. Observational data and patient behaviour allow for analysis of a patient's condition at a much deeper level than in healthcare systems that are based solely on physiological observations. As with most aspects of life, biometrics in conjunction with sophisticated artificial intelligence algorithms is constantly rewriting the healthcare care script with the potential of delivering more accurate, secure and innovative medical systems. When developed, these technologies are projected to be central in transforming the delivery of healthcare services across the world (Sonawani et al., 2023).

2.7.2 AI-Powered Biometric Systems for Authentication and Security

Biometric applications enabled and controlled by artificial intelligence are changing the ways authentication and security are addressed through the use of accurate biometric data and the possibilities of machine learning algorithms. These systems employ private physiological and behavioral characteristics, for instance, fingerprints, face, voice, IRIS, etc., to verify individuals with great efficiency. The use of AI in biometric systems means that the system can assess enormous amounts of data and can process the data in Realtime; this makes the biometric system more stable, fast, and versatile in functional environments. In the general sense, biometrics as an AI application is superior to the password-based security by providing clients with smooth and reliable authentication. For instance, deep learning algorithms can be used for facial recognition carrying out a search for a particular person based on the images of his face, even if the face was tilted, half hidden or photographed under bad lighting. In the same way, voice recognition systems that have been supplemented with artificial intelligence can distinguish between two individuals with very similar voice intonations, thus making for a very secure way of gaining access to a particular system. Apart from the aspect of authentication, these systems are invaluable in delivery of security in healthcare and other sensitive areas. Biometric systems based on artificial intelligence are employed today to preserve patients' data, secure certain zones in healthcare institutions, and track the adherence of health care employees to guidelines. Wearable devices are also on the rise as they allow permanent health check while protecting the data. Physical characteristics that can be used to analyze behaviors like the way a person walks or type on a keyboard are an extra layer of security because if there is a change in a user's behavior, then it is evident that there is an intruder (N., 2019).

2.7.3 Applications in Health Monitoring and Disease Diagnosis

Biometrics based on artificial intelligence are rapidly becoming a breakthrough in healthcare and disease control since they use individual characteristics to detect diseases and monitor patients' health. These systems utilize the most sophisticated machine learning algorithms to mine real-time data gained through wearables, mobile, and diagnostic applications together with offering accurate information of the health status of a specific person. Used for health surveillance, biometric systems are incorporated in wearables, including fitness trackers and smartwatches, for the monitoring of heart rate, blood oxygen levels, sleep, and movement. These indices are analyzed by AI algorithms for determining the presence of any anomaly that might suggest a possible health problem including but not limited to arrhythmias, sleep apnea or respiratory issues. These continuous monitoring capabilities assist in the management of chronic diseases through early detection by the patients, or their healthcare providers before complications arise.

AI embedded Biometric technologies in disease diagnosis; The results have declared that the use of integrated AI in diagnosing diseases has a higher accuracy level especially in the diagnosis of rare and complicated diseases. For example, the facial recognition systems based on AI can identify genetic diseases with the help of specific facial features that indicate Down syndrome or Marfan syndrome, for example. Hormonal biomarkers are also being used to identify neurological and psychiatric disorders such as Parkinson's disease or depression by studying voice changes.

Further, there are applications of artificial intelligence advanced biometric in skin cancer, image analysis in ophthalmology of diabetic retinopathy, and finally, use of gait and movement in tracking up the progress of diseases such as Alzheimer. These systems create patient-specific models and correlate the result with artificial intelligence prediction for creating effective treatment plans and enhanced patient outcomes.

2.8 How AI-powered facial emotion recognition device redefines patient care.

Facial Emotion Recognition (FER) devices powered by AI technology are transformative and innovative for patients' care since there exists unique approaches of measuring, evaluating, and fostering patients' emotional and physical status. These systems detect primary and/or secondary emotions that include happiness, sadness, fear, anger, and stress and other affective states. As a result of the enhanced capabilities of machine learning, FER technology has grown more precise and can now widely be applied in health care. Due to the close relationship between emotional well-being and clinical outcomes these devices are revolutionizing the way care is rendered. A major practical use of FER devices is in behavioral therapy. These systems help clinicians keep track of patients and intervene when signs of emotional distress, mood disorders, anxiety and depression are noted in real time. The presented FER is more objective and accurate than the traditional self-reported methods that are usually riddled with biases or inaccuracies. For instance, FER systems can be used to monitor patients' emotions during psychotherapy or counseling, to help the specialists choose the right approach.

In chronic disease management, FER devices are prescribed for evaluation of the emotional effects of chronic diseases. Emotional stress is a common ailment that results from chronic diseases profoundly affecting the physiology and hinder the healing process of conditions like diabetes, cardiovascular diseases, or cancer. As such, FER devices constantly track the patient's emotional state and offer support in responding to triggering stimuli and subsequently, they offer comprehensive care to patients, which is physical and emotional. Furthermore, FER systems are revolutionizing the patient care in geriatric and pediatric areas. In the case of elderly patients who have neurodegenerative diseases such as Alzheimer's or Parkinson's, FER technology can tell when the patient is developing the early signs of dementia or stress and thus intervene early in order to enhance the quality of the patients' lives. The medical uses of these devices include tracking of emotional signs in children who have difficulties in expressing themselves, which in turn assist in diagnosing the children.

Another twenty-first century area where FER devices are playing a role is in the hospitals. Real-time emotion recognition facilitates to understand the patient's pain, anxiety, or discomfort in the course of procedures or a hospital stay. This data assists clinicians change care plans, analgesia options, or interaction techniques, thereby, improving patient satisfaction and care. For instance, FER devices can ascertain ambience signs of pain in post-surgical patients even when they are unable to direct a word due to machination drugs or other forms of dementia. Furthermore, FER devices combined with AI are improving telemedicine as a whole by revealing the patient's emotional state throughout, during and after a virtual consultation. These systems allow physicians to identify slight shifts in emotion that cannot be observed during video calls and which enhance diagnosis and physician-patient communication. For instance, a patient may have some facial expressions during a telehealth session that show a lot of emotional problems, and the doctor will be forced to dig deeper into the patient's problems that may not be obvious.

In personalized medicine, FER technology is also defining future-oriented, patient-centered health care experiences. Incorporating the patient's emotional reactions into treatment techniques and medication enables the healthcare providers to work at the patient's pace emotionally. While this kind of treatment proves helpful in improving the patient's compliance to the prescribed therapy, it also increases the patient satisfaction. The connectivity of FER systems with wearable gadgets and IoT stations enlarges their applicability in patient care still additionally. For instance, smart health care devices that incorporate FER technology can also always oversee both emotion and physicality of a patient hence giving a full report on such a patient's health status. Hypertension or cardiac disorder patients for instance, FER systems can identify stress signals on the facial features and produce alarm for appropriate medical attention.

However, like with any great potential, there are issues of ethical use, privacy, and culture that FER devices are not immune to as well. Emotion recognition is highly dependent on data and is a considerable challenge when it comes to data protection and permission. Moreover, it is a fact that facial expressions are perceived in different ways in different cultures, so for more societal and unbiased results FER systems should also be trained on different population. Overcoming all these challenges is crucial in order to promote the proper and fair implementation of FER technology in health care. Overall, the facial emotion recognition devices with the help of AI are revolutionizing the patient care by providing real-time, evidence informed approach to the emotional state of a patient. Ranging from psychiatric disorders treatment and chronic diseases treatment to telemedicine and personalized medicine these systems integrate emotional and physical responses to treatment needs into holistic systems. So as to connect patients with health care providers and support teams at the earlies signs of a potential health issue, FER technology can improve the patient's quality of life and the overall effectiveness of the care delivery. With further development in AI expected to enhance the efficacy and flexibility of the FER systems, it should expect incorporation of the innovation in the health sector to expand rapidly marking a new chapter to emotionally intelligent healthcare.

CHAPTER 3

BIG DATA ANALYTICS IN HEALTHCARE

3.1 Unpacking Big Data in Healthcare

Patients can have fewer needless side effects, receive better therapy, and prevent inappropriate care or waste of medical resources if they are precisely matched with medical treatments for certain conditions. Through the investigation of novel medications or the creative or more focused application of already-approved medications, it can also result in new medical therapies (Nicholson et al., 2016). One effective technique for combining many data sources and biologic process research is systems biology. Numerous studies use network models to describe immunological responses and etiopathogenesis, which aid in the discovery of new biomarkers for early diagnosis. Nevertheless, while using such models, clinical data bias should be avoided (Ren & Krawetz, 2015).

Numerous medical devices, particularly wearables, continuously collect data; in an emergency, the huge volume of data generated frequently necessitates quick processing. The deep value from healthcare data (such as public health warnings and personalized health advise) might be maximized through the data fusion of electronic medical records (EMRs) and electronic health records (EHRs), while the value concealed in an isolated data source might be limited (Y. Zhang et al., 2017). Finding structural aspects of the brain in both clinical and scientific contexts is made possible by structural magnetic resonance imaging (MRI), a technique for visualizing a patient's brain that offers detailed brain maps with high spatial resolution and a wealth of high dimensional data.

Through the development of mobile and web applications, patients can now communicate symptomatic queries to healthcare specialists via a server. These smartphone apps might include first aid guidelines; patients could receive directions or emergency assistance for more care. Through the development of mobile and web applications, patients can now communicate symptomatic queries to healthcare specialists via a server. Patients may receive emergency assistance for additional treatment or be referred to the appropriate departments by these mobile applications, which may also provide first aid instructions. To gather and analyse real-time biological signals (such as blood pressure and ECG) from users in different locations, a mobile cloud computing (MCC)-based healthcare system was developed. The mobile device is loaded with a customized healthcare app, and health information is synchronized with the healthcare system's cloud computing service for analysis and storage. Advanced information technology can assist capture big data in healthcare, enabling information exploration to enhance policymaking. A life table can be used effectively to study medical costs and population ageing, which yields data for policymaking (Y. Zhang et al., 2017). As the population ages, so do the expenses related to health care. Big Data technologies are already being used in Japan to enhance healthcare and medical care for the elderly. Through data mining, big data analytics may extract useful information from sizable and complex databases.

3.1.1 Identifying Different Types of Healthcare Data

Clinical language, biomedical imagery, electronic health records (EHRs), genomic data, biological signals, sensing data, and social media are examples of diverse sources of healthcare data. Understanding the connections between various genetic markers, mutations, and illness situations is made considerably easier by the study of genomic data. Additionally, there are a lot of unsolved issues with applying genetic discoveries to personalised medicine practice. Using clinical text mining, unstructured clinical notes can be transformed into valuable information. Techniques for extracting valuable information from vast amounts of clinical writing include information retrieval and natural language processing (NLP). Social network analysis is based on a variety of gathered social media resources, including Web logs, Twitter, Facebook, social networking sites, search engines, and more. It helps uncover new patterns and information that can be used to model and forecast global health trends (like infectious epidemic outbreaks).

Before determining the severity of an illness, appropriate diagnostic techniques must be applied. Table 3.1 (Verma & Sood, 2018) demonstrates a diagnostic system that is used to identify the illness. Table 3.2 (Mendelson & Mendelson, 2017) describes five layers that show health-related personal data. Despite the fact that laws have been the driving force behind technological advancement, data subjects' fundamental rights and privacy should be respected.

Table 3.1:   A scheme for diseases diagnosis in a system

Disease	Diagnostic method	Health measures via IoT
Hypertension	Frequency based; scale based	Blood pressure
Obesity	Scale based	Body weight, blood pressure
Heart diseases	Frequency matching, pattern-matching	ECG pattern
Water borne or infectious disease	Frequency based; scale based	ECG, temperature sensor, Camera pill (gastro intestinal tract)
Stress index	Frequency based; pattern-matching based	Emotiv EPOC sensor, other stress measuring sensors
Respiration index	Frequency matching, pattern-matching	Respiration sensor

Table 3.2:   Datafication layers of personal health data

Layers	Description
Layers1	Internet search, smartphone, purchase, HER, IoT sensors, medical and fitness devices, and healthcare services
Layers2	Clinical and other health-related data in certain formats are gathered, saved, and shared with other parties.
Layers3	Raw data is mostly gathered by private organizations from Layer 1, Layer 2, and additional public and private sources. Either an identifiable or de-identified form of the processed findings is sold or distributed.
Layers4	The data is reprocessed, re-distributed, or re-sold by national governments and multinational business or public corporations for a variety of uses.
Layers5	International agreements and treaties that regulate the privacy protection of health-related personal data

A wireless body sensor network (WBSN) consists of six wireless physiological sensors. The six vital signs—blood pressure, blood glucose, body temperature, heart rate/pulse, ECG, and oximetry—are gathered by the six sensors. Integrating healthcare data—from personal health records to epigenomics—has proven to be a significant challenge. A number of integration techniques have been developed, such as view integration (combining data from different databases), link integration (in a webpage presentation), data warehouse (bringing data into a common data schema), service-oriented architectures (servicing data dynamically at the web in a familiar format), and mash-ups (combining data from multiple Web-based resources for a new Web application). There are some critical aspects or challenges in data fusion that are summarized in Table 3.3 (Capobianco, 2017).

Table 3.3:   Critical aspects in data fusion

Aspect	Description
1	Missing data handling
2	Balancing data from different origins or sources
3	Dealing with inconsistent, contradicting and conflicting data
4	Establishing loss or objective functions and regularization/penalty terms
5	distinguishing between soft and hard data linkages, that is, taking into consideration a random process that generates the data as being subject to the same parameters, or only taking into account covariations, dependencies, similarity/dissimilarity, etc.

3.1.2 The Impact of Big Data on Health Research and Policy

By making it possible to gather, examine, and analyse enormous volumes of data in order to tackle intricate healthcare issues, big data is revolutionising health research and policy. Big data's incorporation into health systems offers previously unheard-of chances to enhance patient outcomes, streamline healthcare delivery, and support evidence-based policymaking. Big data in health research makes it possible to analyse a variety of datasets, such as genetics, wearable technology, electronic health records (EHRs), and population health statistics. This allows the researchers to look at facts, patterns and trends, use the big data to predict possible diseases outbreak, as well as explore the causes of different chronic diseases. For instance, big data has played a critical role in the development of precision medicine, the approach that deploys patient-specific genetic, environmental, and lifestyle information to design treatment. Also, current data from wearable devices and health applications increase the level of monitoring, which helps in diagnosis and disease treatment.

The use of big data is not limited to research but influences formation of healthcare policies. Big data, therefore, is vital in helping policymakers in decision making, development of strategies in public health and evaluation of the performance of health care programs. For instance, in the case of COVID-19 big data analytics was valuable for monitoring the disease spreading, forecasting the healthcare need, and managing the vaccination. In addition, big data will help politicians analyze health inequalities and distribution of treatment throughout the population to provide for those who are at risk. Nevertheless, use of big data in health research and policy also bring about issues that include data privacy and protection. In this case, there are concerns of patient identity while at the same time the ability to combine different data sets is crucial thus ethical practices must be observed. Furthermore, the process of dealing with big data entails efficient computers and a calibrate personnel in this field.

3.2 Leveraging Diverse Data Sources

Employment of different types of big data sources has become a key feature of the contemporary approaches to healthcare advancement as they provide a comprehensive view of a patient, research and decision-making processes. The usefulness of applying clinical, genomic, behavioral, environmental, and socioeconomic data is that with their help, healthcare systems can reveal dependencies between different types of data and work using the integrated information to provide the individualized and effective treatments. Clinical data includes data from patient's medical records and often includes details of patient histories, treatment received, and diagnostic details. When integrated with other data such as DNA sequences this integration enables precision medicine through identification of genetic susceptibilities to diseases and personalizing treatment options. Personal data gathered using wearables and health apps refers to behaviourial data in terms of physical activity, dietary habits, and quality sleep allowing medical professionals and patients to address emerging health issues promptly.

Environmental and socioeconomic information is another dimension when it comes to studying healthcare performance. This correlates with agencies such as air quality, climate and specific neighborhood affecting the rates and progression of diseases, and health disparities affected by factors like income, education and health care access. For example, demographic breakdowns of data on COVID-19 revealed disparities in effects on the marginalized groups and stimulated policies and funding. In research, the use of multiple data sources has made drug development faster and general wellbeing improvement campaigns. Population health research combines population level health statistics with other datasets available at the international level to analyze diseases, forecast epidemics, and plan interventions. For instance, diverse data was used in the development of COVID-19 vaccines where the targeted group was realized and the effectiveness of different vaccines was evaluated.

3.2.1 Harnessing Insights from Electronic Health Records

With its abundance of patient data that can be utilised to improve research, policymaking, and patient care, electronic health records (EHRs) are becoming an essential component of modern healthcare. A comprehensive and integrated view of a patient's medical history, including past and present illnesses and injuries, treatments, prescribed medications and dosages, test results, and imaging reports, is one benefit of gathering and storing all patient data in electronic health records (EHRs). Utilizing such findings creates better patient diagnoses, effective treatments and health care system delivery. Possibly one of the most important advantages of EHRs is the impact it brings to the higher end use of patient care. Immediate access to a patient's records minimizes medical mistakes, including drug interactions and aids in care co-ordination when the patient consults other doctors. Electronic health record systems that integrate artificial intelligence and machine learning can capture data patterns in patients to diagnose diseases early as well as forecast complications. For instance, information from EHRs can be used to develop predictive model for patients prone to certain disease such as Sepsis, Diabetes, Heart Failure among others so as to be treated before time is reached (Topol, 2019).

EHRs are also used for medical research purposes in the same way that other Electronic Health Records can be used. From EHR data, 'big data' of de-identified group health data can be created for disease surveillance, assessment of treatments, and public health research. In the context of COVID-19, EHR data provided useful information on infection incidences and their associations and Their data became valuable to evaluate the outcomes of treatments. Furthermore, merging EHR data with patient's genetic and clinical information and social determinants of health offers the ability to compare how genetic predisposition, lifestyle, and environment factor into disease progression. However, EHRs are not without their problems; some of which include interoperability, accuracy of data and patients' confidentiality. A major challenge common with most healthcare systems is that data does not flow smoothly from one platform to another. Besides, the preservation of patient privacy while at the same time supporting big data analysis presents a major challenge.

Therefore, EHRs are a valuable asset that can be used to gain knowledge that enhances clinical practice, informs research, and advance health policy. If the issues of the interoperability and data security were solved the EHRs have the potential to change the future of healthcare.

3.2.2 The Role of IoT Devices and Wearables in Data Collection

Mostly utilised for patient monitoring and treatment, health wearable IoT devices are also sometimes employed for patient rehabilitation. As was previously said, the sensors record health-related data, and aside from basic analysis, the gadget may transmit the user's or patient's health data online. Additionally, it might get information to let the user make other choices. In numerous applications, wearable technology is linked to smartphones for data analysis before being sent to cloud computing frameworks such as Amazon Web Services (AWS) or Microsoft Azure for data processing, analysis, and storage. Applications for mobile health can be used to display the data that has been analyzed and offer information about the health of the user or patient. Additionally, in therapeutic settings, the data analysis can be used to give the wearer specific instructions, like heating up the body or shocking it.

Health Treatment & Rehabilitation Wearable Systems

Patients with disabilities can preserve and enhance their mental or physical capacities with the aid of IoT rehabilitation equipment. A robot hand receives the wirelessly supplied data after the wearable equipment analyses the bio-potential signals. A machine learning system is then used to evaluate the signals that were collected, providing users with feedback and information regarding their muscle movements. Real-time posture and gait adjustments are made by the user with the help of the robot hand.

Health Monitoring Wearable Systems

Wearable health monitoring devices are divided into four main groups based on the kind of sensors they contain:

1. **Bio-potential sensors,** such as photofluorography (PPG), electromyography (EMG), electrocardiography (ECG), and electroencephalography (EEG).

2. **Motion sensors:** accelerometer and gyroscope.

3. **Environmental sensors:** ultrasound, pressure, temperature, etc.

4. **Biochemical sensors:** transdermal glucose.

A thorough understanding of the patient's or user's health status can be obtained by analyzing the aforementioned signals. The taxonomy of use cases for non-invasive wearable IoT sensors—apart from implanted sensors—is displayed in the picture below.

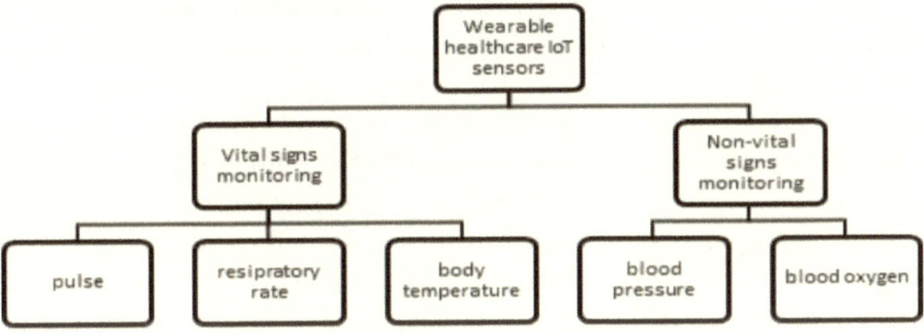

Figure 3.1: Taxonomy of wearable health care IoT sensors

Source: - (John Dian et al., 2020)

Pulse rate monitoring can be performed using wearable devices placed on different body parts, such as the chest, wrist, earlobe, and fingertip. These devices employ technologies like photoplethysmography (PPG), pressure sensors, and radiofrequency (RF) systems. Some wearables are designed to detect changes in heart rate and alert users, for example, through vibrations, prompting timely actions like taking prescribed medication. Multiple sensors are integrated by sophisticated systems to gather information on critical parameters like body temperature and heart rate. These systems can analyses data and provide early warning of conditions like abrupt cardiac arrests, among others, by using smartphones, signal processing methods, and machine learning algorithms.

Specific gadgets incorporate sensors such as ECG monitors into clothing and employ it to monitor the cardiac and respiratory rates constantly. Thermistor nasal sensors are incorporated in wearables to analyze respiratory rate, whereby the temperature changes during exhalation are measured. In chronic ailments for instance asthma, smart IoT based solutions securely transmit respiratory data to the cloud for analysis using features like signal enhancement and encryption.

Another approach includes adhesive hydrogel electrodes which are attached to the chest to detect oscillations arising from breathing. These systems convert collected data into digital form and transmit it through Wireless Ultra-Wideband (W-UWB) system that works within frequency range 3.1 GHz to 5 GHz. Due to small size, low weight, low price, and high-power efficiency, such wearables are becoming more and more popular for long-term health monitoring.

Some of these writers have proposed numerous wearable gadgets that incorporates IoMT technologies to support health monitoring in addition to delivering real-time information. For instance, an IoT smart vest measures respiratory rates in COPD patients during rest while providing continuous home-monitoring. This solution is compatible with e-health electronic platforms hence can be used in remote services. Temperature, an important human vital sign, is usually monitored using thermistor sensors to help in diagnosis of diseases such as hypothermia, heat stroke and fever. A real-time health monitoring cloud-based IoT wearable system has been developed for use with the cloud dashboard as well as with the wearable's display screen. Also, an ingestible tablet-shaped sensor that uses gastric acid to power the sensor to measure the core body temperature transmits data to other devices.

Blood pressure, which is commonly assessed together with pulse, respiratory rate, and temperature, remains a difficult parameter to monitor repeatedly and continuously because there are currently no highly accurate unobtrusive wearable technology solutions. Existing BP devices often come with intrusive or cumbersome configurations like the chest strap ECGs that require wires. Commercial BP wearables have been shown to lack traceability and reliability, which makes this area important for improvement according to the literature. Pulse oximetry wearables are popular for quantifying blood oxygen saturation and change in blood volume by photoplethysmography (PPG) signals. For instance, a non-invasive wearable cardiac monitoring system links pulse oximetry with smart phone and GPS. This device gives alarm when cardiac values go high and it can also switch on alarm using word of mouth.

Wearable devices also continue in the glucose monitoring aspect, including new technologies like smart ingestible drugs that use the near-infrared (IR) to measure glucose levels and send them to smartphones via wireless. In mental health, the IoT-based platforms gather the physiological and behavioral data that determine wellness. Some privacy-preserving features, for example, audio analysis systems, analyse characteristics of speech while not storing the raw utterances making them safe for use in terms of privacy. These examples show the increasing trend of using wearable IoT devices and the expanded roles that these devices can play in health care across an individual's lifetime.

3.3 Advanced Analytics Techniques in Healthcare

Leading the way in the growing application of artificial intelligence (AI) in healthcare are machine learning and predictive analytics. Despite the fact that many of these tools have been around for decades, the current application of analytics to standard medical procedures like screening and diagnosis has raised hopes for using advanced analytics to improve care. For example, it was demonstrated that a deep convolutional neural network (CNN) could be used to achieve excellent accuracy and repeatability in automated screening and diagnosis for retinopathy of prematurity. Eight experts had an average accuracy of 82.0 percent, while their system correctly detected 91 out of 100 photos (91.0 percent) (Brown et al., 2018). In terms of correctly diagnosing melanoma, a CNN also performed better than most of the 58 dermatologists evaluated; its median area under the receiver operating characteristic curve was 0.86 as opposed to 0.79, $P < 0.01$ (Haenssle et al., 2018). Similarly, utilizing cellphones, researchers from Johns Hopkins University created a revolutionary machine-learning method that offers quick, frequent, remote, and objective evaluation of the severity of Parkinson's disease symptoms (Zhan et al., 2018)rater-dependent, and assessed in clinic. Smartphones can measure PD features, yet no smartphone-derived rating score exists to assess motor symptom severity in real-world settings. OBJECTIVES: To develop an objective measure of PD severity and test construct validity by evaluating the ability of the measure to capture intraday symptom fluctuations, correlate with current standard PD outcome measures, and respond to dopaminergic therapy. DESIGN, SETTING, AND PARTICIPANTS: This observational study assessed individuals with PD who remotely completed 5 tasks (voice, finger tapping, gait, balance, and reaction time. These resources play a significant role in consistently high-quality treatment planning decisions. However, the use of predictive models to detect high-risk patients is arguably the most prevalent application of advanced analytics in healthcare. The early identification of individuals at high risk for 30-day readmission or mortality is one potential advantage of these analytical methods. Furthermore, the information obtained from these prediction models has potential as a tool to address urgent public health concerns like reducing adolescent suicide attempts and target scarce resources (Walsh et al., 2018)but clinically practical risk prediction remains a challenge. Screening can be time consuming to implement at scale, if it is done at all. Computational algorithms may predict suicide risk using only routinely collected clinical data. We used a machine learning approach validated on longitudinal clinical data in adults to address this challenge in adolescents. Methods: This is a retrospective, longitudinal cohort study. Data were collected from the Vanderbilt Synthetic Derivative from January 1998 to December 2015 and included 974 adolescents with nonfatal suicide attempts and multiple control comparisons: 496 adolescents with other self-injury (OSI.

Advanced analytics is undoubtedly revolutionizing healthcare at a breakneck speed. The proliferation of algorithms that can simplify complicated jobs, the expansion of the amount of data available, the number and variety of inventors in this field, and improvements in computing power have all contributed to this change. Molecular profiling, remote monitoring, drug discovery, electronic health records, imaging and diagnostics, and billing and fraud protection are just a few of the fields that use advanced analytics.

3.3.1 Descriptive Analytics for Understanding Current Trends

The tremendous but frequently unrealised potential of data has made it a matter of special interest. In practically every area of life, their significance has been demonstrated. While creating the present, data allows for the study of the past and the prediction of the future. Healthcare companies should think about learning about the various methods, resources, and infrastructure that are available to exploit big data, even while profit is not the main driver. Data grows exponentially in the majority of sectors. Large-scale data in healthcare refers to the volume of data that overwhelms a healthcare facility every day. Existing logical techniques can be used to the vast amount of clinical and patient-related data already available, providing a deeper understanding and enhancing healthcare (Mehta & Pandit, 2018). In practical situations, personal data could assist each physician in determining the best course of action for a particular patient. Compared to other industries, the healthcare sector has been slow to adopt big data. huge data operations in healthcare involve gathering, analyzing, and storing consumer, patient, physical, and clinical data that are too huge and complicated for conventional data processing techniques to comprehend. The employment of intricate and advanced sensors in healthcare is an illustration of this large data processing. Consequently, machine learning algorithms and specialized data scientists analyses and interpret large amounts of data (Agarwal, 2015). New approaches are needed by healthcare facilities to solve their ongoing problems, particularly with regard to patient diagnosis and treatment data. Healthcare institutions and organizations must use new technology that can gather, store, and analyse data in order to generate actionable insights in order to address these issues with data volume, velocity, diversity, and validity (Hossain & Muhammad, 2016). Different data strategies should be used in different situations. The goal is to improve patient care and operational efficiency by using healthcare analytics to produce actionable information. The current study reviews prior research and assesses the application of healthcare analytics that are descriptive, diagnostic, and predictive.

Healthcare workers benefit from the use of data analytics, particularly when it comes to disease prediction, diagnosis, and treatment, as well as when it comes to enhancing service quality and reducing expenses. Data mining is thought to help the US healthcare sector save over $450 billion a year (Kakandikar & Nandedkar, 2020). The use of big data in mental health and other fields, including the methodological difficulties of data mining viewpoints, has been the subject of numerous in-depth research (Dash et al., 2019). Rapidly expanding sectors are producing a lot of data, which is drawing the interest of scientists and physicians and necessitating the use of sophisticated data analytics techniques. Healthcare workers may greatly benefit from these methods, which would streamline operations and save a great deal of time, effort, and resources. These techniques may also provide experts with more useful information and knowledge, which would satisfy them. Big data analytics encompasses observation, analysis, prediction, and influence.

3.3.2 Predictive Analytics to Forecast Future Health Outcomes

By utilizing the enormous volumes of data produced by the healthcare ecosystem, data analytics has become a vital element in transforming the delivery of healthcare (Rehman et al., 2022). Healthcare organizations now have access to previously unheard-of volumes of data thanks to the widespread use of wearable technology, electronic health records (EHRs), and other digital health technologies. Such data can be used to provide answers, improve patient happiness, increase operational effectiveness, and save money if it is handled properly. Analytics for healthcare data assists organizations in turning vast amounts of data into information that can be utilized for administrative and clinical decision-making. Finding patterns and connections in healthcare data that would be impossible to find with conventional statistical techniques is made easier for healthcare professionals by the concepts of predictive modelling, machine learning, and artificial intelligence. Additionally, data analytics has played a significant role in organizations' transition from mostly reactive to predictive and preventative healthcare delivery (Razzak et al., 2020). Using historical data and current data, healthcare organizations can predict patients' requirements, patients at risk and provide early care to the patients who are likely to experience a poor health outcome. In summary, data analytics is critical to transforming healthcare through innovation, application to clinical decision making, optimization of patients' health and quality of life and indeed the overall experience of receiving and delivering health care.

Data analytics are techniques of analysis that are used to predict future occurrence and result and predictive modeling is a sub-group of data analytics models. In the case of healthcare, predictive modeling includes the creation of mathematical models that can be used to identify the likely course of a disease a patient is likely to develop, the disease progression, the likelihood of the patient's response to treatment, the probability of readmission to the hospital, and the mortality rate. Patient analytics for outcome prediction is based on the use of multiple data inputs including clinical, demographic, socioeconomic, lifestyle, and genetic data for which the core components are EHR, diagnostic test results, and treatment history. The disparate data sources can be used by predictive models to target high-risk populations, sort patients for interventions, and direct care delivery and resource usages for the best benefit. Some of the most popular methods for the formation of predictive models in healthcare are logistic regression, decision trees, random forests, SVM, ANN, and ensemble techniques. They differ in terms of the level of difficulty in implementing them and the number of computations required of them but all of them are used to estimate future results given present data trends. Clinical decision support for patient outcomes has been described as the next major scientific advance in patient management because of its ability to support population health management, prevention, and early intervention, and individual care planning. Because accurate estimation of patients' status enables proper distribution of resources, coordination of care, and increase engagement with patients, overall health and cost efficiency improves.

Technological developments, changes in legislation and increased understanding regarding the importance of applying data analytics in the healthcare sectors has led to the development of this field. In the past, HDM was mostly a paper-based procedure, which made gathering and analyzing patient data exceedingly challenging. Nonetheless, healthcare organizations started the slow transition to digital data storage with the advent of electronic health records in the latter half of the 20th century, which served as the foundation for data analytics in healthcare today. In the early development of data analytics in healthcare, the primary application was Descriptive Analytics which only analyzed summarized as well as visual data to make inference about patient population, diseases, and healthcare consumption (Batko & Ślęzak, 2022). As the computational capacity grew greater and new types of analytics methodologies emerged, the healthcare organizations began to use the predictive analytics which involves making future presuppositions based on the results of similar prior occurrences. In particular, predictive analytics empowered physicians to recognize those patients who could potentially deteriorate, forecast the further evolution of diseases, and select the most appropriate treatments to enhance patient's lives. More recently, the adoption of 'big data analytics' and artificial intelligence systems which can process massive volumes of information with striking efficiency has expanded the already diverse nature of the healthcare industry even further. Machine learning in particular has showed great potential when it comes to recognizing patterns, drawing conclusions and identifying trends within the healthcare data. Whether it is used for identifying diseases through image analysis in radiology, or for understanding clinical narratives using natural language processing in writing reports, analytics with artificial intelligence is transforming a range of tasks in the provision of care and decision making. Toward future, the developments of healthcare data analytics are predicted to go on and further fueled by technological progress, enhanced access to data and changed healthcare dynamics. The use of data analytics is becoming a major focus for healthcare organizations as they seek to integrate better data into patient care, population health management and operational improvement.

3.3.3 Prescriptive Analytics for Guiding Interventions

Healthcare predictive modeling refers to the ability to use the outcome of a statistical method or machine learning to forecast future occurrences or events. The purpose of predictive modeling is to create equations that would estimate the future state of a patient: inception of a disease, disease advancement, reaction to treatment, reinfection, and death. Predictive modeling as a concept, is all about the use of available data to make predictions on future events or actions. From historical data and, probability analysis, risk indicators can be recognized, populations can be tiered as well as individual patients management strategies developed to enhance patient status and organizational effectiveness (Duncan, 2011). The major steps are data preparing, transforming into features, building the model, testing and finally the model implementation. It is a process of modifying the raw data so that it can be ready for analysis with the help of some tools of data mining. Feature selection refers to the process by which an analyst seeks to determine which variables or features should be included in the model. The act of using the data gathered from prior experiences to train the model using various methods and techniques is known as model training. Model validation involves cross-validating the model or using other datasets to verify the model's accuracy (Powers et al., 2005). Lastly, the used predictive models are employed to predict outcomes on new data with the goal of being used for clinical decision-making in practical scenarios.

Risk assessment and prediction models help the clinician to select patients most at risk of adverse health outcomes and to intervene before such events take place. According to patient characteristics, it is possible to develop accurate prognosis of the necessary treatment and further interventions, and subsequently, to increase the level of patients' satisfaction, as well as the rate of effective treatment (Powers et al., 2005). By using predictive models, healthcare organizations can understand which patients are most likely to gain from specific interventions or services, and hence, determine where resources are likely to yield the most positive results. The use of predictive modeling used in population health to manage disease patterns and risk factors for patient populations to promote effective preventive measures. Performance prediction can make the quality improvement models in healthcare organizations: Clinical data profiling of the patient outcomes may reveal the shortcomings in the organizational structures as well as the practice; Interventions may then be instituted to improve the quality and safety of patient care.

Clinical information such as a patient's demographics, medical history, diagnosis, prescriptions, test results, imaging, and treatment plans can be found in electronic health records, or EHRs. EHR data is a vital source of information for creating prediction models in the medical field since it includes information on a patient's health, illness progression, treatment results, and healthcare utilization. For instance, biometric data, pulse rates, physical activity, sleep patterns, and other vital indicators are continuously collected by smart watches, smart bands, and health sensors. Connected medical equipment and remote monitoring systems that give real-time patient data in non-clinical settings are examples of IoT (Internet of Things) gadgets. IoT and wearable technology provide valuable data for predictive model development, which enables customers' health status to be tracked, any deviations from the norm to be promptly identified, and targeted measures to be taken. Recent trends in next generation sequencing technologies has seen degradation of large quantities of genetic and genomic data such as DNA sequences, gene expression and genetic variants. Molecular genetics and genomics help explain cause of the diseases , risk factors and variation in the response of patients to treatments (Frohnert et al., 2020). The approaches like Genome-Wide Association Studies (GWAS) and Polygenic Risk Scores (PRS) are used to forecast the risk of diseases, distinguish patient groups and, use different therapy strategies. SDOH data includes information relating to the social, economic, environmental and behavioral causes of health and health disparities. Some SDOH data encompasses income, education level, housing, health care access, and food security. Using this approach of data analytics, SDOH data can be used in predictive modeling techniques where social risk factors to health can be identified and health outcomes anticipated so as to come up with the right approach to make improvements on health disparities hence improving the health of the population. With the help of study of different types of data and their analysis, predictive modeling in healthcare allows creating evidence-based, patient-specific, and operational solutions to deliver better patients' health outcomes, enhance the quality and efficiency of care, and support population health management.

3.4 Public Health and Big Data Analytics

Big data analytics is a growing element in the solution of health-related issues in the field of public health. BDA being the analysis of large scale and complicated data, it offers solutions that enhance health, efficiency, and policy decisions. BDA is slowly being integrated into public health systems globally due to the relevance of the solution to the world's challenges including illness monitoring, disease prediction, and resource allocation. Among all the epidemiological applications of BDA, epidemic surveillance and early warning systems stands out as one of the most important areas where BDA has made a major contribution to public health. EHRs, social media, and wearable devices provide real-time information about a population's health, and public health authorities can identify a disease outbreak and take appropriate action. For instance, BDA has been used in the recent past in the analysis of the COVID-19 situation namely informing on the spread of the virus and historical projections for infections as well as containment measures. These predictive models were helpful in defining the necessary priorities and in providing efficient provisions of healthcare (Batko & Ślęzak, 2022).

Beside epidemiological surveillance, BDA enables individually tailored prevention measures based on population pooled data with regard to disease risk and behavioral factors. This type of information is crucial in the development of effective preventive strategies that eliminate excessive rates of chronic diseases including diabetes and hypertension. For instance, predictive analytics help in not only identifying the populations at a higher risk of getting the diseases but also in taking preventive measures (Dash et al., 2019). Another area where BDA is revolutional is health equity and social determinants of health. Big data is utilized by public health investigators in the analysis of differences in access to and use of health care and services among population subgroups. This helps policy makers to correct the imbalances which the health needs of the deprived group of people. For instance, through GIS, BDA can show the distribution of healthcare services in the rural areas and suggest developmental changes that can be made to close the gaps.

In addition, big data's ability to combine data from other sources is useful for health assessments that capture more complete pictures of people's health. People's genes, their activity levels, what they eat, and air quality can be measured and analyzed to get a view of health determinants at multiple levels. Such an approach makes it possible to practice precision public health, that is, address the needs of a particular group (Batko & Ślęzak, 2022). However, the use of BDA in public health has its advantages and disadvantages as will be discussed next. Privacy and security issues are still major challenges as the gathering and processing of such information raises some ethical questions. Further, obtaining information from various sources, use of analytical tools to combine them varies and may not be easily affordable especially in developing countries. In order to optimize the use of BDA in public health the following challenges need to be overcome (Batko & Ślęzak, 2022).

Therefore, Big Data Analytics makes a valuable contribution in decision-making processes of public health and its artful application contributes to equity and individualized approaches to interventions. Addressing current challenges will help the public health systems to better leverage BDA to improve healthcare and population's health.

3.4.1 Enhancing Real-Time Surveillance Systems

Big Data Analytics (BDA) has emerged as the most radical tool currently being implemented in the fight against health challenges in the public health domain. BDA offers useful insights to human health, resource utilization and policymaking from big-scale and complex datasets. BDA is gradually being incorporated into health systems in many countries for problems like disease monitoring, epidemic forecasting, and resource allocation. In terms of public health BDA has made a very positive impact in the areas of epidemic surveillance and early warning systems. EHRS, SNS data, and wearable technologies help public health authorities identify disease outbreaks, and thus, react promptly. For example, in the case of the COVID-19 outbreak, BDA was instrumental in monitoring the spread of the virus and comes up with estimates of infection rates and how they should be controlled. These predictive models were used to determine the areas that need most attention and where amount of healthcare resources should be applied.

Apart from disease surveillance, BDA empowers individuals to receive targeted health promotion by providing population-level data of risk factors and behaviors. Such insights are necessary when one wants to formulate prevention and control measures for the conditions such as diabetes and hypertension. For instance, predictive analytics can help healthcare providers to recognize populations that are at risk and act before a problem occurs (Jeon et al., 2024)

The fourth area that BDA is revolutionary is in health equity and social determinants of health. Big data helps public health researchers understand where different demographic groups are accessing or not accessing healthcare and their outcomes. This in turn empowers policymakers to harness the right strategies to ensure that underprivileged groups get the correct care that they deserve. For instance, BDA can show where healthcare is accessible in the rural regions and suggest the changes in the infrastructure to close the gap. Also, big data's capability to incorporate data from different sources helps in holistic evaluations of the health sector. An example where big data can be harnessed includes pulling data from wearable devices, genomic analysis, and environmental sensors to study correlation present between genotypes, behaviors, and the environment affecting Health. This conceptual framework makes it possible to dispense precision public health in which interventions are made depending on the population's requirements (L. Zhang et al., 2024).

However, there are challenges in implementing BDA in public health. The most important limiting factors are privacy and data security since the collection and processing of PHD are unethical. Furthermore, consolidation of data from various sources is complex and time-consuming, and a valid analysis might not be available in low resource settings. It is crucial to meet all these challenges to optimally realize BDA in enhancing public health (Iqbal et al., 2021).

As a result, Big Data Analytics can be considered as an effective weapon that is shaping public health and helps to make decisions in advance, increase equity, and provide individualized approaches. Recognizing current issues, public health systems can improve further application of BDA in improving the health care delivery and population health.

3.4.2 Predicting and Containing Epidemic Outbreaks

Another important area of using big data in public health is the ability to forecast and prevent further expansion of epidemic diseases. The use of real time data, analytics and predictive models can enable health organizations to closely track, prevent and contain the spread of infectious diseases appropriately. Through proper utilization of these capabilities, the public health agencies will be in a position to make sound decisions, use available resources well and therefore reduce mortality rates. Big data analysis allows combining large amounts of data related to health, collected from different sources by using such data as EHR, social media accounts, applications for mobile devices, and IoT devices. This is used to detect pest patterns, trends and correlations as have been established as showing indications of an outbreak. As an example, quick increases in the flu's symptoms reported at clinics or conversations about certain illnesses on social media can indicate an epidemic's onset. These are the kind of insights that are core to early intervention (L. Zhang et al., 2024). Forecasting epidemics is one of the primary uses of PM, and the results of the analysis have significant implications for health care decision-making. By the application of machine learning, models can have ability to scan and learn from the past epidemic records and also has the ability to predict and consider live parameters such as population density, travel schedule, climate change, and immunization frequency. These models do not only forecast how a disease might progress, but also, where, and to whom it might pose a significant threat.

For instance, during COVID-19, big data models were applied to identify areas most likely to be infected and to contain cases or provide vaccination (Jeon et al., 2024).

Managing to contain epidemic outbreaks also depends on the data analysis when it comes to distribution of resources. It assists the heads of public health in forecasting the requirements for medical equipment, beds as well as, the health personnel in the affected areas. Also, it helps the authorities to track the movement and interaction of infected people with other citizens using mobile telephony data or other means. This makes it easier to quickly quarantine anyone who may have come into contact with the virus and thus greatly lessen the transmission rate (Iqbal et al., 2021). Similarly, IoT based real-time monitoring system supplies latest information on environmental and biological factors responsible for disease transmission. For example, IoT sensors can point to either air quality or vectors such as mosquitoes in malaria-endemic areas to warrant fumigation or vaccination respectively (L. Zhang et al., 2024).

3.4.3 Leveraging Big Data for Global Vaccination Campaigns

The big data is also instrumental in planning, executing and even in the monitoring of vaccination exercises all over the world. Of all the applications of Big Data Analytics for Public Health, the following are crucial in addressing logistical challenges, increasing vaccine coverage and the overall effectiveness of immunization: Health care records, social networks, Satellites data and reports and real time reports. Another important benefit of big data in vaccination drives is that big data can be used to obtain important demographic information regarding the population and disease incidence, as well as the infrastructure of the vaccine distribution channels. The evidence shows that health data, along with geospatial data, can be used to detect regions and populations who are underserved or potentially at risk. For example, it can show the districts with low immunization cover or the zones that are vulnerable to epidemiological flare-ups due to inadequate immunity pool. These insights facilitate adequate intercessions, pointing out those individuals in need of vaccines while preventing wastage and improving resource utilization.

However, it must be noted that big data plays an important role in the tracking of vaccines, which are also needed to be managed. Supply chain analytics can keep tabs on storage conditions and movements, track distribution in real time, and discourages spoilage via the application of temperature sensors in

IoT devices. This helps vaccines to remain effective and it also guarantees that they get to the intended place in the right state. In the COVID-19 pandemic, digital platforms helped governments and organizations to monitor vaccine distribution in different countries and ensure fair distribution to low-income countries using organizations such as COVAX. Big data also improves the control of vaccine effectiveness and safety. Monitoring systems collect data on adverse reaction and/or events after vaccinations and review the reports from practice care givers and vaccinated individuals. Machine learning algorithms analyze large data sets in search of relatively low incidence but high-risk adverse events, thereby informing regulatory action and disseminating information to the public.

In addition, big data assists in the fight against a major challenge in attaining high levels of immunization; vaccine reluctance. Thematic analysis of social networks allows for the detection of misinformation circulation and evaluating people's attitude towards vaccines. Such knowledge enables public health authorities to develop more effective, context-specific awareness raising initiatives, reject fakes, and strengthen people's confidence in vaccines. Last but not the least, the last benefit of big data is that all aspect of vaccination campaigns such as the level of coverage, effectiveness, and perception can be assessed through the large amount of accumulated data. Such feedback mechanism can enable health agencies to modify strategies and correct gaps in as they progress to ensure better immunization.

3.5 Ensuring Security and Privacy in Healthcare Data

Since digitization is the watchword in this generation, the protection of health care data is paramount in order to instill confidence among the members of the society as well as protect health information that is sensitive in nature. The use of big data in the health care sector enhances its value in terms of; The diagnosis of diseases, The treatment of diseases and Disease control. But it also poses the issue of how to ensure that patient data does not fall to the wrong hands, get leaked or misused. Solving them demands strong security measures and Privacies frameworks. Healthcare data is especially at risk as it is valuable for use on black markets, and, therefore, targeted for cyberattacks. Securing an application's data is essential for protecting it from malicious access and, at the very least, encrypting information prior to storage and data transfer is an obvious must. Tools such as the end-to-end encryption work in a way that if the data was intercepted, it cannot be read without the decryption key. The Role-Based Access Control (RBAC) is another working method for controlling the measure of the data access granted to people within an organization because it restricts data access tentatively to the personnel categorized according to their responsibilities as a way of reducing internal misuse.

The security should be audited periodically and the access logs should be monitored to check for areas that can be exploited. Virtual means can identify and prevent any malicious activities, which makes the health care systems even more secure. Furthermore, Staff training programs remain essential so that healthcare workers are aware of their responsibilities concerning the safeguard of information of the patients in special regard to EHRs. Adherence to regulations pertaining to data protection is another crucial element. Therefore, it is permissible to state that a legal foundation for data protection is provided by laws such as the General Data Protection Regulation (GDPR) in the European Union and the Health Insurance Portability and Accountability Act (HIPAA) in the United States. Openness is required by these standards; a healthcare organization cannot collect and distribute patient data without the consent of the patient.

Big data systems can also apply anonymization and de-identification approaches to ensure patient physician data privacy while not reducing the usefulness of the data to researchers. For instance, masking of personal data by codes or use of statistical data decreases the incidence of privacy infringements while at the same time promoting health research.

3.5.1 Best Practices for Safeguarding Patient Information

The protection of the patient data is always embraced as one of the core competencies in proper and safe medical practice. With EHRs and digital systems continuously being adopted in many healthcare organizations, good measures should be put in place to ensure that such important information is protected from being violated, or used inappropriately. Technological, procedural, and regulatory security measures to protect patients' information: technology, policy, and legal approaches.

Encryption can be viewed as one of the main technological controls that translate sensitive information into an unrecognizable form if the key to decoding the information is not correct. This measure is critical for securing data in motion and in repose especially in cloud based healthcare systems (Abouelmehdi et al., 2018). As important as data security is device security, that is, the protection of the gadgets that are used to access patient's medical records, through setting complex passwords, use of identification codes, use of protective hardware, among others. Daily software updates and patches reduce risks that hackers might use to access an organization's system.

Healthcare institutions must also use role-based access control (RBAC) that limits data access the same way depending on the position of the user. RBAC only allows access to those users who require the information thereby reducing the cases of internal misuse (Shenoy & Appel, 2017). Moreover, daily audits of access logs also help to increase security since all deviations in users' activity are revealed during the audit.

However, beside the technology the human factor remains the key. Of great importance is sensitization of healthcare staff on their policies regarding data privacy and or cyber security measures which may occasionally be infringed by a staff through ignorance. For instance, they should learn how to notice phishing scams and how to manage patient's information effectively. Another integral element of protecting the patient's information is compliance to the regulations. HIPAA in the United States prevents the use of patient information in any unauthorized ways and offers definite recommendations for reducing risks. Similarly, the General Data Protection Regulation (GDPR) in Europe makes patients data processing to be done with the consent of the patient.

To increase extant privacy measures, medical organizations can use de-identification strategies that scrub or occlude identifiable information to maintain patient privacy but allow analysis. This is why more recent technologies like blockchain are also appearing as reliable for handling health care data due to their distributed and immutability.

3.5.2 Navigating Legal and Ethical Challenges in Data Use

Any given acquisition, application, or sharing of healthcare data presents cogent legal and ethical questions especially given the increasing importance of digital health and big data in healthcare. The use of information technologies in research and patient care is pervasive with EHRs, wearable devices and AI; it is crucial for data to be used appropriately and within the law. One of the key features of addressing these challenges is the need to strike a fine balance between the interests of patients on one hand and health innovators on the other. A legal issue is the protection of clients/ patient's data especially with reference to the HIPAA for the United States and GDPR for European countries. These frameworks require that patient information must be obtained, managed and transmitted in a secure process, but at the same time, give patients control over their data. But, the integration of such regulations in healthcare systems is not a simple process because while working to protect the information from unauthorized access, it needs to be made interoperable for better health care outcomes.

In some cases, ethical factors play a vital role when using healthcare data, this create the need for the following. Some of the questions that arise and put ethicality of the healthcare under threat include questions to do with informed consent, ownership of data, and use and misuse of, often sensitive, information. For example, patients may not understand how their data is used in other related activities such as research or marketing which may reduce their trust in a particular healthcare facility. Ambitious efforts to enhance the quality of data practices are needed to address these ethical dilemmas, and that includes transparency in data practices and the enhancement of consent. In addition, there are questions regarding the ethical use for AI and machine learning in healthcare, such as the issue of bias. Machine learning models could be potentially a double-edged sword since models trained from biased data resources are likely to compound bias in care delivery for vulnerable groups. Regulatory and moral standards should be created to increase the openness and fairness of AI systems in their decision making (Elendu et al., 2023).

In conclusion, the use of healthcare data faces legal and ethical issues which can only be addressed through collaboration of policymakers in health care, health care providers as well as technologist. We can then be sure that, by chasing high legal standards and promoting ethical practices, healthcare systems can use data to their advantage and advance care delivery, all the while maintaining the trust of patients.

3.5.3 Addressing Cybersecurity Threats

With a rise of digitally oriented health systems used for storage and processing of highly personal and private patient information, the healthcare industry becomes one of the most attractive targets for cyber criminals. Hacking attacks including ransomware, data leaks, and phishing threaten not only patient's data but also patient's healthcare. As such, the threats require firm cybersecurity measures, anticipatory action, and protection of digital assets. The EHR and connected devices are among the most critical areas of weakness that healthcare cybersecurity face in their endeavor to secure the sector. EHRs contain huge amount of personal, medical and financial data which makes these systems interesting for hackers. Also, the new technologies like Internet of Things (IoT) which comprises more connected health devices including the wearable health monitors and smart infusion pumps pose several new entry points for the attacker. These integrated systems require complex protection measures including robust encryption, multiple layers of identification and continuous immediate threat detection and mitigation measures (Bala et al., 2024).

Ransomware attacks are especially dangerous in healthcare because they leave the organization unable to function due to locked data. For example, those in major health care facilities such as hospitals have suffered from situations that a patient's records cannot be retrieved during an emergency hence endangering life. To this end, healthcare organizations need to embrace constant data backup, network separation and educating their employees on how to recognize and deter phishing incidents which are usually the precursor to ransomware attacks. Another fundamental issue in cybersecurity is compliance with HIPAA for patient's data protection in the United States using technical, physical and administrative controls. Organizations also have to perform risk management and penetration testing on the System at least once per year.

Thus, cybersecurity is not only a technical issue but a key aspect of patient protection and public confidence in healthcare. By implementing an overall strategy to addressing the shortcomings in cybersecurity health care organizations can reduce their exposure and safeguard the privacy of patients' information.

3.6 Operational Efficiency Using Big Data

Big data analytics is fast becoming the key to attaining efficiency in the operations of organizations by identifying and managing processes, as well as making effective decisions. This is defined as the large amount of data being produced from different sources for instance, sensors, social networks and transactional systems. With this information, organisations and businesses are able to identify areas of wastage, and even forecast changes that are likely to occur. A major field where big data plays a role is in the supply chain where business intelligence assists in supply chain planning, demand forecasting and thus leads to cost effective and efficient delivery of services. For example, data from sensors in real time can track stocks, alerting the organization to situations where stock is low or high and using this data to estimate the stock a business's needs before having to place large orders. Further, big data analytics enhance the process efficiencies where; analysts locate areas of congestion in the various activities being conducted. Business entities can use such models to identify problems that may occur and affect their functioning. This is well illustrated in manufacturing where predictive maintenance models make predictions on when equipment could fail and set time for maintenance to be done to help avoid failure thus lowering the repair costs. In addition, big data ensures that organisations deliver customised services to its customers, which increases their loyalty. In view of this, customer behavior analysis ensures that products and services being offered are of most importance to customers hence leading to high patronage.

In the transport industry, big data is applied in the management of route, fuel, and logistics, which boosts performance in the industry in an enormous way. Logistics companies can use past traffic flow data and current information flow to minimize delivery time and fuel consumption leading to an ecological added value and cost reduction. Big data therefore, when combined with sophisticated analysis tools, becomes a critical competitive advantage in improving organizational performance across industries by increasing intelligibility, decreasing expenses, and increasing service quality (Bag et al., 2020).

3.6.1 Predicting and Preventing Hospital Resource Shortages

Managing and forecasting hospital resource deficiencies is one of many real-life uses of big data analytics in the healthcare industry. This paper provides general information about hospital resource management including staff, medical supplies, equipment, and beds that are key operational tools. The use of big data analytics can predict future shortages by using data on their usage history, demographics of patients, seasonal changes and other practical streams of data. These insights enable the healthcare administrators to plan and actually know ahead of time when resources might become scarce and lead to a compromise on the care of the patients. Such values as patient admission rates, the schedule of surgeries, and emergency visits can be analyzed with help of predictive analytics. Such factors help hospitals to forecast demand for their services during particular days and weeks, and, therefore, better allocate expected number of patients. For instance, if the analyzing of data provides information that the number of flu cases rises in some months, it will be possible to strengthen the staff, order extra equipment and make sure that there are enough beds for patients. Further, the models may assist hospitals in managing inventory consumption and identifying inventory depletion tendencies to restock before it happens (Chrimes et al., 2017)Victoria, BC, Canada.

The proof-of-concept implementation tested patient data representative of the entire Provincial hospital systems. We cross-referenced all data profiles and metadata with real patient data used in clinical reporting. Query performance tested Apache tools in Hadoop's ecosystem. At optimized iteration, Hadoop Distributed File System (HDFS.

There is one specific example, for example, the application of big data for the prognosis of staff deficiency. Administrators in organizations, in this case, hospitals can look at data tracing staff absenteeism, staff workload and patient's acuity to predict staff requirements in future and areas of shortages. Thus, hospitals can set more effective shifts for their workers, find temporary staff in case of need, and even some of the functions can be fully or partially robotized which free up their workers for more important tasks. As for equipotent, big data can locate idle equipment and recommend where the equipment should be deployed in different departments that require their usage most. For example, if certain diagnostic equipment is highly demanding but underutilized in another section, it is best to redeploy so that it can help overcome inefficiencies. Big data also enable the accurate calculation of the time that a patient is likely to be discharged so that appropriate arrangements for the hospital beds can be made.

Hence, the predictive analytics based on big data improves the hospital resource management cutting down on costs, and elevating the hospital's patient care; it also guards against problems that may lead to shortages that threaten the facility's operations.

3.6.2 Optimizing Patient Flow and Bed Utilization

Managing patient and bed traffic is a major challenge from an organizational perspective in most healthcare organizations especially hospitals. This goal is achieved through the use of big data analytics which help to give real time information on patient mobility, bed status and treatment times. Using data on the number of patients that a hospital receives and send to other facilities and the time taken between, hospitals can eliminate areas of congestion, optimize the number of beds allocated and used. Hospital occupancy can be managed using big data, in terms of patients admitted, discharged and those transferred from one ward to the other. The demand for patients can be predicted with the use of patterns old data, seasonal rate, and emergency cases. This helps the hospitals to be able to know how many patients are expected to come in at a particular time, hire enough staff, get the right resources and make the right patient flow process. For example, there is a way to predict high workload and guarantee the presence of beds in essential sectors, including the emergency department or intensive care (Al Harbi et al., 2024).

Further, it also assists the patient discharge process by identifying when patients can be discharged by considering their vital status making reductions of waiting time for new patients possible. Using data regarding patients' records, it is possible to predict the time required to stay in the hospital – this information will be useful for effective organization of beds. Furthermore, there is an opportunity in using the predictive analytical tools to estimate patients' likely to cause a long wait before discharge, so that, appropriate measures are taken to avoid blockages that result in lack of available beds. Another example includes, hospitals can also manage their inventory of beds effectively with required real time data that is needed to shift patient from any department to other where beds are vacant. For instance, if there are many patients in a certain ward, there will be a way of transferring these patients to other wards that have many empty beds, thereby avoiding congestion and ensuring that resources are utilized properly. In addition, use of information on the time taken to discharge patients and the expected time before new patients arrive optimizes the turnaround time of elective operations to help reduce bed holding period (Bonamigo et al., 2023).

In conclusion, incorporating big data into patient flow management optimizes patient flow within a healthcare organization by minimizing wait time, thereby increasing the effective use of available resources that include bed space; improving patient results at the same time decreasing organizational costs.

3.7 Big Data for Personalizing Healthcare Experiences

Big data has a revolutionary function in the management of patient care as well as has the potential of providing customized patient care solutions to health care providers. Using large quantities of data from EHR, wearable devices, genetic information, and feedback, the healthcare systems can get better insights of the need of each individual patient to enhance the quality of the final results and patients' satisfaction. Personalized health care is based on evidence from research to develop the care plans that the patient needs based on their medical record, genetic profile, behavior, and constant health information. Big data analysis helps the system to discover patterns of diseases that will help in diagnosing and treating the diseases involving big data by improving the management of chronic diseases and advancing drug therapies. For instance, through big data, it is possible to learn how certain genetic make-up of patient may have an effect to certain medicine hence reducing the side effects in cases of medication while at the same time enhancing the effectiveness of medication in treatment (Viceconti et al., 2015).

In addition, big data allows for prescriptive analytics, whereby the needs of patients are expected before being required. Through the examination of prior performance, such models can anticipate disease development, advise on prevention, and indicate to clinicians that a client may be at risk of a stroke or heart attack. This approach is not only efficient in the provision of health care services but also facilities patient's involvement in managing their health. Furthermore, the combination of big data with patient engagement solutions, including Mobile applications and Health monitoring gadgets improves the patient's care plan. These tools give the patients and healthcare givers the feedback immediately and can help in close monitoring and treatment in case of an emergence of a problem.

3.7.1 AI Algorithms for Tailored Treatment Plans

Artificial intelligence applications in healthcare are focused on the creation of individual patient treatments to achieve the best results. These algorithms employ the patient's records such as medical history, genetic makeup, habits and ongoing physiological condition to design personal health management plans. Some of this information can be studied by AI systems and the patterns and correlations that may not be apparent to clinicians can be revealed by the AI systems, making treatments more refined and individual. This model of AI in creating customized treatment interventions is best illustrated in Precision medicine. AI can analyses a patient's genotype and then estimate how the person will react to certain treatments so that the chosen drug or therapy is the most effective. This decreases trial and error in the prescription of drugs and gets rid of a number of side effects making the overall success rate of treatments higher. AI models also help them in the adjustment of the dosage of medication which is made more accurate using machine learning algorithms that keep learning from new patient data and improve on the dosages affected by patients' reactions to the treatment plan (Salam & N, 2024).

Another important practice where artificial intelligence is making difference in the treatment planning is the application of predictive analytics. Based on the past experiences, including diagnosed and treated illnesses,

AI can estimate how these diseases, including cancer, diabetes or heart diseases will develop. It helps the healthcare providers to prevent aggravation, by modifying the treatment schedules before the condition gets out of hand. In the case of chronic diseases, the AI algorithms are able to track the patient's health data from wearables and make necessary changes to his or her treatment plan constantly, as opposed to the traditional model of having to wait for a routine appointment in order for the doctor or nurse to review the patients' conditions and then adjust the treatment plan if necessary (Sharma et al., 2024). Moreover, AI is useful in a context of rational distribution of health care resources whereby treatment plans are not only individualized, but also economically efficient. AI can offer insight into the possible patient reactions and disease progression, therefore help to determine which specific actions should be taken for the best and quickest outcome, avoiding multiple unneeded treatments. Therefore, it can be concluded that decision-supporting systems based on AI are not only making patients' life better but also promoting more efficient and sustainable healthcare worldwide.

3.7.2 Real-Time Adjustments to Care Based on Data Insights

The use of analytics to make real time decisions regarding patient care is one of the ways that healthcare is changing for the better as patient needs are better addressed. Using real time data, the healthcare provider can make changes that are informed in the same day to the patient's care and therefore guarantee that the care the patient is receiving is optimal and based on the patients' current state of health. Perhaps one of the biggest advantages of real time data analysis in healthcare is the efficiency at which patients' conditions can be closely watched in real time. The constant flow of information from wearable technology, sensors and electronic health record generate fresh information that allows clinicians to modify care approaches immediately. For example, in critical care units, real time data helps the health care professionals monitor such things as heart rate, blood pressure and oxygen level. That is why, if any of the patterns are found to be different from normal, changes to the patient's medication or treatment program can be made on the spot to avoid further risks or speed up the healing process if necessary (Wills, 2014).

Furthermore, real time data is useful in altering care plans of chronic diseases. Diabetes patients can for instance have continual glucose monitoring, where information is transmitted to care givers instantly. If a patient has a high or low blood sugar level treatment modalities can quickly be changed averting complications and enhancing patient wellbeing. Thirdly, real time data can improve the flow of patients in emergency situations and enhance patient care by making rapid assessment of the severity of condition of the patient. It also helps in decreasing the healthcare costs since it is based on data. Some of these benefits include reducing the number of invasive procedures performed and hence reducing their attendant complications and costs; and averting complications by identifying them earlier in the course of a disease, which makes care less expensive as a system.

3.7.3 Enhancing Patient Engagement Through Customization

Personalized care is at the heart of the patient engagement strategy, one of which is through customization. This paper also establishes how big data is a critical element in personalizing health care delivery, increasing patients' roles and engagement. By processing a large volume of patients' data, healthcare providers can create individualized plans of treatment, which will correspond to patient's health histories, needs, and their behavior in particular, which means that the treatment process will be more individual. These are; demographic information, medical history and lifestyle information, all of which has to be understood in order to begin customization. For instance, big data tools may draw recommendations based on age, gender, income, and other treatments. The described strategy is not limited to patients' medical requirements; it also considers their features of communication and use of digital technologies. Targeted communication allows for more efficient delivery of information, that can provide comfort to patients during their experience. For instance, the use of communication through technology that can include but not limited to, reminders or health tips and can be personalized to enhance compliance with the regimes or a healthier lifestyle to enhance the results.

It also allows healthcare providers to monitor and analyze the level of patient engagement in real time, too. For instance, using real time data, a provider can assess the extent to which patients are compliant to prescribed treatments, and change it as required in real-time. It makes the process of patient involvement more effective and dynamic, because it engages patients in their treatment process instead of just reacting on the treatment.

Also, the use of big patient data with artificial intelligence and machine learning to support the more precise prognosis of possible patients' health problems and more individualized approaches to addressing them before they become potentially life-threatening. Measures of this nature do not only have positive impacts on health since they enhance positive health but also facilitates increase patient understanding and satisfaction hence enhancing patient-physician interaction. In general, the healthcare service customization with help of big data is a promising approach to increase the quality of clients' experience and bring the services closer to the clients' preferences thus improving the health and satisfaction of the recipients.

CHAPTER 4

ETHICAL, LEGAL, AND SOCIAL IMPLICATIONS OF AI IN HEALTHCARE

4.1. Ethical Concerns in AI Applications

Artificial intelligence (AI) is a term applied to a machine or software and refers to its capability of simulating intelligent human behavior, instantaneous calculations, problem-solving, and evaluation of new data based on previously assessed data. AI heavily influences many industries and fields, including agriculture and farming, manufacturing and production, autonomous vehicles, fashion, sports analytics and activities, healthcare, and the medical system. This technology has the power to impact the future of the industry and human beings, but it is a double-edged sword.

AI applications in healthcare have literally changed the medical field, including imaging and electronic medical records (EMR), laboratory diagnosis, treatment, augmenting the intelligence of the physicians, new drug discovery, providing preventive and precision medicine, biological extensive data analysis, speeding up processes, data storage and access for health organizations. However, this field of science faces various ethical and legal challenges. Despite tremendous strides made in the field of AI in communities, and its role in improving the treatment process, it is not accessible to all societies. Many low-income and developing countries still do not have access to the latest technologies. It should be noted that the ethical dilemmas, privacy and data protection, informed consent, social gaps, medical consultation, empathy, and sympathy are various challenges that we face in using AI. Therefore, before integrating artificial intelligence with the healthcare system, practitioners and specialists should consider all four medical ethics principles, including autonomy, beneficence, nonmaleficence, and justice in all aspects of health care.

4.1.1 Privacy and Data Protection

General Data Protection Regulation (GDPR) was first enacted by the European Union (EU), as it amended the privacy legislation in other countries, such as the US and Canada. According to these regulations, all personal data and the activities of foreign communities and companies are processed by the union-based data processor or controller in order to protect the information of natural persons with sufficient protection. In the United States, the Genetic Information Non-discrimination Acts (GINA) is an organization that prohibits employers from discriminative decisions according to the genetic health information of individuals. In fact, the role of AI in healthcare is to analyze consumer health data and medical device images, improve diagnoses and outcomes, as well as a helpful role in accelerating health research activities.

In addition, social media, as part of AI, play a vital role in disseminating health news or medical advice, especially in pandemics. However, these can be ostensible positive aspects of AI, and ensuring the safety of the patients' data is still a significant concern when using robots:

- In healthcare, current laws are not enough to protect an individual's health data.

- Clinical data collected by robots can be hacked into and used for malicious purposes that minimize privacy and security.

- Some social networks gather and store large amounts of users' data, for instance, individuals' mental health data, without their consent, which can be helpful in the marketing, advertising, and sales of these companies.

- Also, some genetics testing and bioinformatics companies, which are not legal or closely monitored, sell customer data to pharmaceutical and biotechnology companies.

4.1.2 Informed Consent and Autonomy

Informed consent is a process of communication between a patient and health care provider, which includes decision capacity and competency, documenting informed consent, and ethical disclosure. According to the definition of ethical responsibility, patients have the right to be informed of their diagnoses, health status, treatment process, therapeutic success, test results, costs, health insurance share or other medical information, and any consent should be specific per purpose, be freely given, and unambiguous. Concerns about this issue also increased with the rise of AI in healthcare applications. Based on the autonomy principle:

- All individuals have the right to get information and ask questions before procedures and treatments.

- Patients should be able to be aware of the treatment process, the risks of screening and imaging, data capture anomalies, programming errors, the privacy of data and access control, safeguarding a considerable quantity of the genetic information obtained through genetic testing.

- Patients may refuse treatment that the health care provider deems appropriate.

- Patients have the right to know who should be responsible when these robotic medical devices fail or errors. The answer is essential for both patient rights and the medical labor market.

4.1.3 Social Gaps and Justice

Another problem that threatens societies following the development of AI is the social gap issue. In all countries around the world, with every development, discovery and invention, people face greater social inequality and less social justice. Although AI improves the accessibility to more information about science and technology, world events, climate changes, and politics around the world, it exacerbates social inequality, as mentioned below:

- Automation and advanced economies have widened the gap between developing and advanced countries.

- Many people lose their jobs as robots grow and develop.

- Bookkeepers and managers in different communities could lose their jobs with the increase of automated systems, and there will be a considerable decrease in salaries.

- The rise of surgical robots and robotic nurses in healthcare environment, operating instead of surgeons and caring for patients instead of nurses, threatens their future job opportunities.

4.1.4 Medical Consultation, Empathy, and Sympathy

Integrating artificial intelligence (AI) with all areas of health care seems difficult and impossible. Due to uniquely human emotions, human and medical robots might not evolve together in a short time. Physicians and other care providers should seek consultation from or provide consultation to their colleagues, which is not possible in autonomous (robotic) systems. On the other hand, it seems unlikely that patients will accept "machine-human" medical relations instead of "human-human." Doctors and nurses are expected to provide treatment in an empathetic and compassionate environment, which will significantly affect the healing process of patients. This will not be achieved with robotic physicians and nurses. Patients will lose empathy, kindness, and appropriate behavior when dealing with robotic physicians and nurses because these robots do not possess human attributes such as compassion. This is one of the most significant negative aspects of artificial intelligence in medical science. For instance:

- In Obstetrics and Gynaecology, any clinical examination requires a sense of compassion and empathy, which will not be achieved with robotic doctors.

- Children usually experience fear or anxiety as they engage in healthcare settings and meet professionals. Their behavioural manifestations are lack of cooperation, withdrawal, and aggression that could be uncontrollable with the new robotic medicine system.

- The use of medical robots in psychiatric hospitals may adversely affect patients who have severe psychiatric disorders.

4.2 Protecting Patient Privacy in AI Systems

Advances in healthcare artificial intelligence (AI) are occurring rapidly and will soon have a significant real-world impact. Several new AI technologies are approaching feasibility and a few are close to being integrated into healthcare systems. In radiology, AI is proving to be highly useful for the analysis of diagnostic imagery. For example, researchers at Stanford have produced an algorithm that can interpret chest X-rays for 14 distinct pathologies in just a few seconds. Radiation oncology, organ allocation, robotic surgery and several other healthcare domains also stand to be significantly impacted by AI technologies in the short to medium term. In the United States, the Food and Drug Administration (FDA) recently approved one of the first applications of machine learning in clinical care—software to detect diabetic retinopathy from diagnostic imagery. Because of this rapid progress, there is a growing public discussion about the risks and benefits of AI and how to manage its development. Many technological discoveries in the field of AI are made in an academic research environment. Commercial partners can be necessary for the dissemination of the technologies for real world use. As such, these technologies often undergo a commercialization process and end up owned and controlled by private entities.

In addition, some AI technologies are developed within biotechnology start-ups or established private companies. For example, the noted AI for identifying diabetic retinopathy is developed and maintained by start-up IDx. Because AI itself can be opaque for purposes of oversight, a high level of engagement with the companies developing and maintaining the technology will often be necessary. The United States Food and Drug Administration, are now certifying the institutions who develop and maintain AI, rather than focusing on the AI which will constantly be changing. The European Commission has proposed legislation containing harmonized rules on artificial intelligence, which delineate a privacy and data principle of organizational accountability very similar to that found in the European General Data Protection Regulation. Other jurisdictions like Canada have not completed tailoring regulation specific to AI. AI remains a fairly novel frontier in global healthcare, and one currently without a comprehensive global legal and regulatory framework.

AI have several unique characteristics compared with traditional health technologies. Notably, they can be prone to certain types of errors and biases, and sometimes cannot easily or even feasibly be supervised by human medical professionals. The latter is because of the "black box" problem, whereby learning algorithms' methods and "reasoning" used for reaching their conclusions can be partially or entirely opaque to human observers (Hashimoto et al., 2018). This opacity may also apply to how health and personal information is used and manipulated if appropriate safeguards are not in place. Notably, in response to this problem, many researchers have been developing interpretable forms of AI that will be easier to integrate into medical care. Because of the unique features of AI, the regulatory systems used for approval and ongoing oversight will also need to be unique.

A significant portion of existing technology relating to machine learning and neural networks rests in the hands of large tech corporations. Google, Microsoft,

IBM, Apple and other companies are all "preparing, in their own ways, bids on the future of health and on various aspects of the global healthcare industry (Powles & Hodson, 2017)." Information sharing agreements can be used to grant these private institutions access to patient health information. Also, we know that some recent public–private partnerships for implementing machine learning have resulted in poor protection of privacy. For example, DeepMind, owned by Alphabet Inc. (hereinafter referred to as Google), partnered with the Royal Free London NHS Foundation Trust in 2016 to use machine learning to assist in the management of acute kidney injury. Critics noted that patients were not afforded agency over the use of their information, nor were privacy impacts adequately discussed. A senior advisor with England's Department of Health said the patient info was obtained on an "inappropriate legal basis". Further controversy arose after Google subsequently took direct control over DeepMind's app, effectively transferring control over stored patient data from the United Kingdom to the United States. The ability to essentially "annex" mass quantities of private patient data to another jurisdiction is a new reality of big data and one at more risk of occurring when implementing commercial healthcare AI. The concentration of technological innovation and knowledge in big tech companies creates a power imbalance where public institutions can become more dependent and less an equal and willing partner in health tech implementation.

While some of these violations of patient privacy may have occurred in spite of existing privacy laws, regulations, and policies, it is clear from the DeepMind example that appropriate safeguards must be in place to maintain privacy and patient agency in the context of these public–private partnerships. Beyond the possibility for general abuses of power, AI pose a novel challenge because the algorithms often require access to large quantities of patient data, and may use the data in different ways over time. The location and ownership of servers and computers that store and access patient health information for healthcare AI to use are important in these scenarios. Regulation should require that patient data remain in the jurisdiction from which it is obtained, with few exceptions.

Strong privacy protection is realizable when institutions are structurally encouraged to cooperate to ensure data protection by their very designs. Commercial implementations of healthcare AI can be manageable for the purposes of protecting privacy, but it introduces competing goals. As we have seen, corporations may not be sufficiently encouraged to always maintain privacy protection if they can monetize the data or otherwise gain from them, and if the legal penalties are not high enough to offset this behaviour. Because of these and other concerns, there have been calls for greater systemic oversight of big data health research and technology.

4.2.1 Data Encryption and Anonymization Techniques

Data encryption and anonymization techniques are foundational to ensuring privacy and security in information systems, particularly in sensitive fields like healthcare, finance, and government data management. Encryption is the process of transforming information from its normal form, that is readable form (plaintext) into an unreadable form (cipher text) known to unauthorized users by use of keys. Current algorithms for symmetric encryption are the Advanced Encryption Standard (AES) and asymmetric systems like the RSA encryption system. These methods are indispensable to secure messages en-transit and at-rest. Data anonymization on the other hand aims at preserving privacy by eliminating identification of identity of users from datasets for use while avoiding invasion of privacy. Some of the forms of anonymization are data masking, pseudonymisation, generalisation and suppression. For example, pseudonymization substitutes PII by pseudonyms so that the data can be valuable in analytics without compromising privacy.

Another beneficial feature of using both encryption and anonymisation is that privacy is achieved in accordance with HIPAA in the USA and GDPR in Europe. Both frameworks require high security measures for the data protection, for the processing, storage, and transfer of the private data.

Newer advancements in these technologies focus on the enhanced anonymization of the dataset through Differential Privacy that adds random noise to the data set while preserving data utility while minimizing privacy risk. Further, the progress in methods such as homomorphic encryption enables computations of encrypted data without decrypting them reducing exposure in data handling. Such technologies are of great importance in healthcare systems where the aspect of privacy is highly important, and sharing of data safely can lead to improved diagnostic work and results. However, as it will be seen, implementing encryption and anonymization is far from being a walk in the park. Encryption algorithms increase computational load thus reducing the processing speeds and when data is anonymized it can be reverse again if not protected well. Solving these issues implies constant improvement of the approach and compliance with all the standards regarding data protection.

4.2.2 HIPAA and Other Compliance Standards

HIPAA stands for Health Insurance Portability and Accountability Act, and it is at the foundations of healthcare data protection regulation. HIPAA was passed in the year 1996, for the protection of patient health information in terms of confidentiality, integrity and availability. Its Privacy Rule defines information privacy requirements for people's medical records and other PHI in order to facilitate the exchange of health data necessary for quality treatment. The Security Rule adds to this by addressing administrative, physical and technical measures to protect ePHI. For instance, it requires risk assessments, and control for data encryption and access to guard sensitive information from unauthorized users (Feld, 2005). Apart from HIPAA, there are other rules regarding standards the healthcare organization has to meet depending on the location and type of data. The GDPR applicable in the European Union has sufficient measures to protect data that is categorized as personal especially the health data. In GDPR consent is highlighted alongside; data minimisation and the right to access and erasure of personal data. In the same manner in the research study, the ethical standard set by the Belmont report facilitates the ethical use of health data. It is crucial to adhere to these standards, particularly with the rise in the use of digital systems and constant threats of cybercrimes.

These standards require that healthcare providers and organizations respond by putting into place compliance measures. Some of the features of extensive compliance include providing staff with certain training, auditing frequently as well as coming up with policies on how to handle data. For instance HIPAA regulatory standards demand that healthcare institutions should have disaster preparedness plan, log-in reviews for malpractice and periodic technology updates (J. Q. Chen & Benusa, 2017). It also important to note that compliance frameworks not only protect patient's trust but also help in creating operational efficiency, and innovative environment. For instance, compliance with HIPAA allows for effective exchange of information for telehealth services leading to better access and outcomes. Also, failure to adhere to the set measures faces heavy consequences, financial and reputational, which makes compliance crucial.

Thus, compliance standards' development will remain the key as more and more healthcare systems go digital. Technologies that are new include artificial intelligence and cloud computing, the use of which requires new methods of regulating risks while tapping into opportunities. Therefore, organizations need to employ effective compliance management solutions that support the use of these emerging technologies; to sustain an optimum level of protection of patient data in line with international standards.

4.3 Legal Challenges in AI Healthcare

The use of AI in health care has brought several legal issues, due to the innovation and at the same time complications it brings. Perhaps one of the most significant legal questions is to know who is to blame when the AI-based solutions and products behave incorrectly or are non-responsive. For example, when an AI-based diagnostic system fails to read medical data correctly, it becomes ambiguous to determine whether the medical practitioner, the software designer, or the implementing organization is responsible? This is made worse by the fact that most AI algorithms are black box systems meaning that it is hard to tell where exactly something went wrong. Another important issue is data privacy because health care AI systems work with large amounts of personal and often sensitive patient data. It is mandatory to adhere to laws including the GDPR in the European Union and the HIPAA in the United States, but it is also difficult, especially where cross-border transfer of data occurs is required. These regulations are the strict measures for data protection, for getting the informed consent and for anonymizing the patients' data but their practical application may be costly and legally complex (Gerke et al., 2020). This also extends to legal issues especially in regard to ownership and protection of intellectual property (IP) rights in AI healthcare. Who exactly owns AI generated innovations – whether it is the developers, the health care organizations, or even the AI itself is still unknown? Also, since the regulatory policies are generally not updated to match the fast-growing AI industry, there are questions regarding the procedure for approval of AI-based health care devices and systems. For instance, in some regions, absence or ambiguity of the rules for checking and certifying adaptive learning AI systems hampers their validation and approval prolongating their clinical adoption (Da Silva et al., 2022)similar innovations in governance (law, policy, ethics.

Further, bias in AI systems creates biases in results, which creates legal risks to the institutions regarding to fairness and equality in the management of health care services. These biases which can be derived from bias training data unfairly favour certain groups, against the anti-discrimination laws. Solving these issues needs cooperation of legislatures, technologists and care-delivery entities to establish strong and effective legal frameworks and proactively and ethically apply AI in the healthcare sector.

4.3.1 Liability in AI-Powered Decisions

Determining who is responsible when things go wrong in a system driven by artificial intelligence is considered one of the biggest legal questions in the field of medicine. Computer aided diagnosis, treatment planning and medical image analysis are some of the new technologies that has brought new dimensions in identifying the parties responsible. Bearing the risk has been traditionally assigned to the human subjects – the physicians and healthcare institutions. However, with the introduction of AI, all these lines are blurred, and no one knows who is to blame when an AI system is failing, whether it is the healthcare provider, the AI developer, or the institution that is implementing such a system.

One of the major problems is related to the fact that many of AI systems are "black box" and the ways they operate are not easily discernible. The former are capable of generating high levels of accuracy although the process is questionable and it is hard to determine an error's root cause. When an AI system makes a mistake of diagnosing a patient, fault may be split across the system design, deployment, and usage. Some courts may use a legal precedent, such as medical malpractice or product liability laws, to settle such cases, but they are not well prepared for addressing the AI algorithm's ability to make decisions independently.

Moreover, a new dimension has emerged in terms of the standard of care in tussles involving AI. When physicians are engaged, they must follow necessary procedures to ensure that what the system is providing is accurate. If a physician simply relies on the AI generated diagnosis or recommendations and proceeds to issue a wrong one, then he or she will be held vicariously liable for negligence. Nevertheless, if a physician decides to go against an AI that gives a correct recommendation, they too will be held legally responsible. This brings two fold risk which makes it important to have adequate training and at the same time health care personnel should be in a position to have faith in these AI systems but at the same time should have a basis to decide.

The other legal issue that is in question is the organizational negligence. It is therefore on the institutions implementing the AI systems to conduct tests, validate for errors and ensure that errors, when they occur, are reported. If it is not done it may lead to institutional liability. Further, a growing trend is where those developers of AI systems are being held under the product liability laws especially where there are defects in the system that lead to harm. This brings to light the question of whether there should be joint responsibility in which several individuals may be made to answer.

It is crucial to adapt the existing legal systems to cover the features of AI these are its autonomic operations, reliance on data and the shifting standard of reasonableness. Despite the potential benefits of AI for healthcare, governments and regulatory agencies need to set rules for acceptable uses and shift the responsibility while doing so – AI has to be safe.

4.3.2 Intellectual Property in AI Technologies

As with most emerging novel technologies, the protection of IP in AI technologies remains more of a work in progress than anything else, and brings up questions and issues that are difficult to address within the confines of traditional legal systems. AI systems are designed and constructed by software developers from data offered by data providers and used by end users which poses complex questions of ownership, authorship, and rights. Once AI technologies have started to transform such sectors as healthcare, manufacturing, and creative industries, knowledge and its protection, as well as commercialization of intellectual property assets becomes a necessity (Estupiñán Ricardo et al., 2021). A major challenge in AI-generated IP is establishing the copyright protection for the work done by or through AI systems. Previous copyright legislation apply to works with human authorship, but given that current AI systems are increasingly becoming independent, the question arises of whether such content can be considered original. The Copyright Directive has been met with responses that range from assigning copyright to developers or owners of the AI system to the idea of new frameworks that recognize the function of the technology. For instance, the "personality" and creativity of the generative AI models contradict the traditional legal perception of authorship.

Similarly, patents of AI technologies involve a similar social concern as other technologies, for instance, on matters of inventiveness and non-obviousness. As most AI systems are based on data sets and sophisticated computations, assessing the novelty of such system may be problematic. Formal ownership rules, where much attention is paid to tangible objects, such as patents, do not directly fit into intangible products such as, for instance, machine learning models or neural networks. Ownership issues should also be tackled by developers particularly when the work being done is a combined venture or an open source tool. These challenges show that the current patent systems require replenishments to respond to AI innovations. Trade secrets and data protection also have a critical place in the AI IP management actions. Most companies depend on trade secret as means of protection rather than patents, as many organisations consider their algorithms and data as their primary asset. However, this creates problems in enforcement since the foe can easily get hold of the confidential information or reverse-engineer the format.

The new theoretical paradigms promote a fair, equal, and flexible AI and IP regime. This study aims at helping policymakers close the gap between these legal categorisations and the newer, more complex characteristics of AI to provide intellectual property laws that will foster innovation without hindering competition. Another aspect that will also be important as most of AI development has gone international is the cooperation internationally in setting and enforcing the standards.

4.3.3 Regulatory Barriers to AI Implementation

Some of the most compelling issues that organizations encounter while advancing in the adoption of artificial intelligence are regulatory barriers. The growth of AI technologies has been more dynamic than the formulation of rules and regulations governing their use thereby putting AI technology in a state of disconnection with regulation. This situation creates problems related to compliance, legal risks and ethical usage that render it challenging for organizations to implement AI as desired and responsibly (Lombardo, 2022). Certainly, one of the main obstacles is the ambiguity and the absence of a uniform approach to regulatory policies in different countries. Few nations have developed sound legal frameworks to cover AI moral, legal, and functional aspects. Variation in the laws governing data protection, and ownership of ideas, as well as allocation of risks make it difficult for firms that operate internationally. For example, the GDPR prescribed some specific regulation of data usage in the European Union that might not always be compatible with the necessities of satisfying AI systems that need substantial data for set learning (Onitiu, 2023).

A related concern is the adoption of a paradoxical role of regulation as both a driver and a constraint. On one hand, the rules which are clear and effective can serve as artier allowing to minimize risks of unethical usage of AI systems. However, too many or ill-formulated norms may become an obstacle to the creation of new products, as developers have to satisfy numerous state standards. For instance, freedom of use of artificial intelligence is limited in the health sector by regulations in some jurisdictions which may hinder the introduction of important innovations that will save lives. Another significant challenge is the quality and quantity of data needed for AI development and use within an organization. AI systems have a large amount of data and the laws that apply to data acquisition, processing, and utilization can affect the use of AI. In case data protection policies relating to sensitive personal information for example, the co-ordination is poor thus making it difficult to harmonize practices across sector. In addition to these, other ethical issues such as privacy and surveillance also make it hard for companies and organizations to adopt the use of data-driven Artificial Intelligence (Lombardo, 2022).

Also, distribution of losses in AI operations is still uncertain and topical in many legal frameworks. This is particularly true in high-risk applications such as self-driving cars and diagnostic algorithms raising questions of who is responsible when things go wrong. codified law does not fit well when decisions are made by artificial intelligence instead of natural one. This reality puts organizations on the back foot when it comes to AI deployment as they do not want to be caught up in a legal battle (Lee et al., 2023). The regulatory barriers are however worsened by the fact that there is no effective coordination of the stakeholders. Some of the problems are that governments, regulatory bodies, and industries stakeholders act independently, and therefore their efforts to address AI governance are scattered. It is crucial for multiple stakeholders to collaborate in order to shape those regulatory policies based on technological environments and opinions from all parties.

These barriers have to be addressed taking a complex approach. Thus, the society requires robust flexible policies that will address the social value of the IOT technology while at the same time containing the vices of use. Global polices and practices can be harmonized through public private partnerships between governments and institutions. Besides, improved information about AI advantages and its promotion of transparency can minimize social concerns and contribute to trust formation. Therefore, it can be concluded that although barriers from the regulatory point of view are substantial, they are by no means insuperable. The experiences from various countries demonstrate that with synergistic actions and more flexible policies it is possible to promote the use of AI safely and fairly.

4.4 Social Impacts of AI Adoption

Artificial Intelligence (AI) integration is revolutionarily transforming global society with special emphasis on the economy, education, healthcare, and the workplace. Another drastic effect is the change of the nature of workforce. AI systems can directly operate processes previously conducted by humans and this brings questions on owners and employers of those jobs. Research has it that automation will impact low skilled or repetitive jobs hence social imbalances and rather inequalities (Tai, 2020). But at the same time AI also opens new possibilities to personnel development and new types of professions appear that are closely connected with the need for changes in educational models to meet the requirements of the jobs connected with AI. In education, the use of AI technologies improves adaptive learning activities in education since it adapts to the learner's learning styles and speed. The above systems enhance the educational system in the unserved areas by offering them AI tutors and learning tools. Nevertheless, there exists a disparity in the use of these technologies as a result of the digital divide, where socio-economic differences limit the equal use of these technologies. They also express concerns about data privacy and surveillance because the large amount of data accumulated by such systems threatens civil liberties if not used responsibly.

Health care organization has received significant advantages from AI implementation, including accurate diagnostic, differential treatment approaches, and enhancing the flow of healthcare facilities. Some examples of AI-based technologies include: Predictive analytics that help organizations to identify patients who are likely to develop a certain disease before they show symptoms and to allocate resources appropriately. However, more questions are raised regarding the patients' data privacy and the potential for bias in AI applications. Research shows that accuracy is inherit in training data and that this results in prejudice in health care for the minorities. To address these problems, there is a need for many regulatory measures that will guarantee fairness in operations. AI has many functions in the economy. On one hand it sparks innovation, helps increase efficiency and promotes economic growth as well. AI technologies enhance supply chain, customer relationship, and technical decision making in different sectors. On the other hand, AI adoption is still uneven across sectors and regions which increases inequality in economies, and may leave small companies who do not have financial capital to put into the AI technology outcompeted. To enhance the positive impact of this disruptive technology, the governments and policy makers must devise means to democratized the AI.

The implementation of AI in society also affects interaction in relationships and moral values. With the increase use of AI in decision making processes in areas such as policing and finance the issue of who is to blame in case of a wrongdoing arises as does the issue of fairness. Furthermore, AI has become a part of people's life, and the implementation of AI requires refining the principles of privacy and consent, which are typical for conventional technologies. These potential decisions may lead to the usage of deep fake technologies, spread of false information or any other negative consequences which is why the topic requires proper regulation and public awareness.

Organizational and individual consequences of AI implementation are relative to each other. People's encounters with artificial intelligence technologies, including virtual agents or chatbots, change communication patterns and shape related attitudes. Although AI is convenient, risk of over-reliance of students on AI degrades the development of problem-solving skills. Additionally, there is an existing perception of bias regarding the attitude towards artificial intelligence where some people consider it as an unsafe innovation that will jeopardize the liberty of people while others for various reasons welcome the innovation. Summing up, AI usage has a wide range of social implications; the advantages are groundbreaking, and the difficulties should be addressed. Solving these problems requires cooperation of different governments, business stakeholders and civil society in order to make AI as a tool for social progress but at the same time preserving human dignity and equality.

4.4.1 Shifting Dynamics in Doctor-Patient Relationships

The adoption of AI technology in the healthcare domain has already impacted health care doctor-patient relations in very many ways. Typically based on trust, empathy and clear communication, such relationship is enriched by the possibilities emerging from the use of AI in diagnostics, treatments and delivery of the services. Technology tools include cognitive computing, predictive modeling, and decision support through intelligent virtual health assistants, can analyze a large volume of data to interpret and transform ideas, understand complex conditions, and determine the most effective course of action regarding a patient's health care. Though these advancements enhance productivity and patient results, the interaction between the physician and the patient is changed. Of all these changes, the most outstanding is the use of artificial intelligence in support of diagnostic work. New age artificial intelligence models can understand and interpret complex medical data to minimize diagnostic mistakes and provide live suggestions. This can enable the patient to have more information regarding the conditions they are suffering from and enable the patient and the medical personnel come to a consensus on the management of the diseases. However, it may also threaten the educational monopoly in the doctor-patient relationship and may contribute to the erosion of the traditional doctor-patient rapport (Qian et al., 2024). Physicians need to find ways of assuming an AI support role and still be able to retain the physician-patient humane relationship.

AI also has effects on the interaction between a doctor and a patient. Telemedicine applications and virtual health assistants also grant people an immediate opportunity to talk to a doctor and receive usual treatment, sparing time for direct meetings. As much as these technologies increases access and convenience, they decrease the interpersonal touch that is very important in patient satisfaction and compliance with treatment regimens. For example, patients who are using only the AI-based interaction tools will be devoid of their physician's interpersonal contact and, thus, have less trust in the treatment process. In addition, because of the intelligibility of AI algorithms, there are the ethical and emotional concerns at the same time. Some patients may not be able to either comprehend or even belief in the decisions made by the system in critical or emergency situations. Such approach nurtures skepticism and resistance to AI assisted care and makes the role of doctors intermediaries that translate AI recommendations into a comprehensible form for patients. There are also issues with data privacy and shortcuts in AI solutions that point out physicians to consider the problems with dataset bias or with ethical issues in AI systems that can harm minorities and other people with decreased protection.

The new doctor-patient relationship in the age of AI also implies the changes in the roles and competencies of doctors. Apart from being diagnosticians/treatment providers, physicians are being expected to become coordinators and translators of AI-generated knowledge. This requires a twin strategy of attaining technological mastery while at the same time foster interpersonal relationships to minimize the disconnection of human touch when it comes to healthcare service provision. In conclusion, this paper finds that although AI offers enormous benefits to healthcare delivery with the potential to transform doctor-patient relations, these relationships incur new intricacies. Yet, to govern these changes, physicians need to become adept at functioning with AI and work AI into practice in a manner that does not erode patient-centric attitudes and relationships, and that guarantees that implementing AI is supplementary to human care, not a replacement for it.

4.4.2 Addressing Socioeconomic Disparities in Access

Artificial Intelligence (AI) is advancing at a constant pace in today's world, and it opens great opportunities in almost every industry, it also reveals some significant problem in AI accessibility. As a result of the SES, the accessibility and uptake of AI technologies have made a reproduction of existing inequalities. The above causes are an indication that every segment within society should be provided with equal opportunities that will be given by the incorporation of artificial intelligence. There is one overwhelming reason behind these inequalities, and it is the digital divide. Leveraging AI solutions entails the use of resources such as internet, advanced devises, and IT literacy all of which are still a preserve of the high-end income earner. For instance, in the area of learning, low income students are even struggling to acquire AI based learning solutions thus exaggerating the difference in achievement between the rich and the poor [4]. Likewise, industries that utilize AI for efficiency of operations might disadvantage little enterprises unable to afford AI by incorporating their enterprises.

To address these gaps, the government, and private organizations need to focus on efforts that aim to improve the availability of AI. Such are the sponsored projects to lay down the Internet connection in rural regions, combined with the low-cost AI applications. Also, the campaigns promoting digital literacy should cover excluded groups, which must learn how to interact with AI. For example, the availability of the open-source AI software, or mixed public and private partnerships in funding and developing AI tools and models can make these resources a level playing field (Capraro et al., 2024). Another key approach is equity in the creation of Artificial intelligent models. This result implies that the AI is a product of its training data and therefore can have pre-biased preference towards less privileged customers. This prolongs historical disparities in employment, credit, and healthcare to mention a few. They are required to follow ethical AI practices and even ensure that the datasets fed into the AI are diverse. Law makers should set rules that require organizations using the systems to conduct fairness checks and make sure that the AI systems do not provide unfair outcomes.

Disparities are also eliminated through education. Training programmes in AI courses should be geared towards reskilling the underrepresented groups in order to allow them to benefit from the emerging AI based economy. Bringing all the scholarships and mentorship program and an inclusive curriculum will enable people with such backgrounds to embrace and advance in the exploration of AI. Thus, IT is clear that, while AI offers virtually unlimited opportunities for the improvement of various aspects of society's functioning, efforts to mitigate negative socioeconomic effects that AI can cause or deepen are also needed. AI developers, industries, and schools should act in harmony to promote a message that AI should unite people and not divide them and that everyone should be able to benefit from it.

4.5 Workforce Implications of AI

Artificial Intelligence (AI) is rapidly being adopted across the world in workplaces and this is changing the global workforce system in a fundamental way. The automation and optimization of processes, improvement of decision-making processes, as well as predictive analytics brought by AI is now changing industries and everyday work profiles. Even though AI can bring many advantages, like higher performance and productivity, it can pose some threats, including high risks of job losses, shortage of qualified workers, and concerns of ethical nature. The automation impact of AI in the workforce is arguably one of the most discussed topics up to date. Sometimes, AI systems can help the employees avoid fatigue because it can perform repetitive and mundane jobs, which won't allow individuals to be imaginative, think about strategies, or even interact with others in a meaningful way. For instance, self-service bots can engage in simple and repetitive questions as human operators work on complicated cases. Nonetheless, calls for the automation of some roles have been deemed as a cause for job loss most evidently in manufacturing, logistics, and administrative roles. According to the recent 2020 survey, 82% of various positions in different industries have been altered by AI and that many of these positions have been either redesigned or completely eradicated (Zirar et al., 2023).

AI is also revolutionising what it means to have skills for future occupations. With technical work becoming automitable, the interpersonal and people skills like empathy, flexibility, teamwork, etc., are getting valued more and more. Also, there are certain technical skills, which workers require to have such as data analysis skills, machine learning, and AI programming. The adoption of AI technologies will require organizations to promote upskilling and reskilling in order to produce the needed human capital. Research on the subject suggests that upskilling is not just an outcome of AI but a necessary process for success in an AI-based economy (Morandini et al., 2023).

However, AI is now affecting leadership and decision making in organisations. Information is power and because AI systems can go through a large amount of data and come up with a comprehensive report, leaders can take better informed decisions faster. However, for this transformation to work, organisational leaders need to have a firm grasp of AI technologies so that they can adequately understand AI-driven interpretations. The decision-making process is becoming more collective, meaning that the human and machine collaboration is becoming essential for the best result. Data findings show that the companies that approach AI to support instead of displacing human employees are likely to perform well in this new environment.

One more implication of accepting AI option is the effect on employees. On one hand, AI means automation, which contributes to the rationalization of work and thus can lead to decreased stress levels arising from monotonous tasks; on the other hand, it can create job insecurity and workers' senselessness. A survey of employee's digital well-being demonstrates that such issues must be resolved by creating positive attitudes towards inclusion and openness among employees. Promoting the active involvement of the employees in the processes of the integration of AI in the workplace and stressing on the partnership between humans and AI can help to overcome adverse outcomes. Other factors that closely relate to the workforce implications of AI are ethical ones as well. Biases in AI algorithms, therefore, result in discrimination in hiring, promotions, and even evaluation of employee's performance. It is important to make the AI systems fairly balanced and accountable so as to make the employees trust in the various systems. Failure to do the above means that organizations have to put in place proper governance measures for the detection of AI biases. Moreover, ethical AI application crosses the loop of data privacy where the companies need to secure the employee data and the AI needs to reveal how it makes decisions.

Nevertheless, AI has relevant potentials for changing the directions of the workforce. It frees up time in roles that used to be too bogged down by operations to be creative and innovative in work that they do. For instance, in the medical field, AI tools help the physicians do their work more efficiently by helping in such tasks as appointment booking and record keeping. Likewise, in finance, AI can perform computation of transactions and identification of fraud while employees focus on value addition such as planning and selling to the clientele. AI has also potential effects on the workforce in gig economy and remote working as well. AI platforms help in the process of placing workers in certain jobs, managing their schedule and even give feedback to gig workers in real-time. However, this shift has brought new concerns relating to employment status, employment benefits and the status of gig workers whether they are employees or independent contractors. These are issues which policymakers cannot afford to overlook in order to develop fair working conditions for employment in an environment with artificial intelligence.

The nature and impact of AI on the workforce therefore require proactive treatment that is also inclusive. This include the culture of learning, the human-AI collaboration model and ethical practices. There is also a part of governments and educational establishments since they have to develop the policies and programs for transformation of the workforce with the help of AI. For instance, collaborations between industries and universities can fill this gap through offering programs that offer workplace-specific training. In conclusion, AI is the tool that revolutionizes the workforce across industries, open the new opportunities and 'darkens' the new challenges. Hence, when adopting AI, organizations can leverage the benefits and work around the risks, by investing in upskilling personnel, practicing ethical AI, and implementing inclusion policies. As technology progresses we need to work towards the integration of AI into the work force recognizing that human resources remain important as does development in AI systems.

4.6 Building Public Trust in AI Healthcare

The process of building public trust regarding AI in health care is rather complex because its foundation is a key to successful implementation and use of AI technologies. It is crucial for integration as trust lays down the foundation for decision making in healthcare since these decisions influence patients' lives. Establishing this trust can be achieved through enhancing the ethical, technical and social issues that are involved in the processes and regulatory frameworks by promoting applicability of clear processes, policies, gentle patient engagement, and education. The degree of transparency together with accountability is a critical aspect in the development of trust. Be explainable AI systems have to be and clinicians and patients have to be able to understand why an AI system arrived at a certain output. The process of explain ability also reinforces trust in AI recommendations to enable the adoption of these in clinical practices. It also helps to make ethical decisions since the use of algorithms is made clear about how they arrive at particular decisions.

Lack of transparency may make AI systems look like a black box, and this does not encourage both clinicians and patients to accept such systems (Steerling et al., 2023).

Supervisory authority also takes a central task as well as the role of a catalyst On this regard, It is therefore imperative to note that regulatory oversight also takes a central task as well as the role of a catalyst. It is clear that governments and healthcare institutions need to develop high standards of how AI technologies are to be developed, tested, and implemented. These frameworks should protect patient autonomy, privacy, and ensure that everyone stands to benefit from artificial intelligence. Certification to international standards like the GDPR and HIPAA showcases an organization's commitment to ethical practices and protection of patient's information. The other area of trust-building is when the patients and the clinicians participate in the creation of AI systems. Engaging end-users in the development of the AI solutions guarantees that the tools are useful, and can easily be used to solve real-life health care problems. For instance, the involvement of patients and healthcare workers during the development of AI research improves the system ownership hence credibility. It has also been established that the participation of the users enhances the functioning of AI, and also ensures that users have confidence in the final version (Banerjee et al., 2022). Education serves as the means of narrowing the gap between the creation of the AI and the clinicians as well as the general public. This causes skepticism or over reliance that hinders AI's effectiveness since people go in with wrong perception about it. It will require positive reinforcement to get the public to understand the true capabilities of AI and their shortcomings to ensure that there is not a unrealistic expectation placed on the technology. Another important consideration is that healthcare providers should also be trained about how to work with AI and understand how to use its recommendations – the idea being not to disintermediate the industry but to turn healthcare providers into the drivers of AI. For instance, the book – Ethics and Governance of Artificial Intelligence in Healthcare – advances the idea of trust within the development of AI technology by showing that it begins with the creation of awareness within stakeholders.

In particular, security and privacy of the data affect trust in building. This means that patients require certain guarantees about their protected health information not being ill-used or compromised. It does this by embracing state-of-art encryption as well as anonymization mechanisms, not forgetting governance mechanisms of data. Compliance with privacy regulation causes confidence in the authenticity of the AI due to various data breaches that erode the public's trust in technology (Arora et al., 2021). One of the other approaches relates to making AI fair and neutral, or in other words, a question of non-bias. Therefore, Healthcare AI needs to be built in a way that will provide the same benefits to all in society despite the color of their skin. Traces of systemic biases can be reflected through ways of data collection as well as algorithm creation leading to discriminations within the care approaches provided to marginalized groups. Adopting stringent testing procedures to flag and remove such prejudices enhances confidence since the process shows a dedication to diversity.

Last but not the least, trust building, in this case, entails the construction of the virtuous cycle of continuous improvement and effective accountability. AI systems should always be audited and adjusted to the new developments in medicine and other related social requirements. Providing feedback and grievance mechanisms corrects maladies that may arise within implementing the technology, and enables stakeholders to have their say on the progress of the project. Trust is not an end state but a developmental one: it needs consistent work to be built and maintained. Overall, to establish public trust for AI healthcare application one must include the key elements of transparency, regulation, stakeholders, teaching, security, equity, and continuous enhancement. Focusing on these aspects will contribute to using AI to the maximum effect to improve patients' experience and change the practices within the healthcare industry. This means engaging the technology experts, policy makers, healthcare providers and consumers, to make trust a process component of AI implementation.

4.6.1 Educating Patients and Providers on AI Benefits

Incorporation of AI in medical practice and patient care is one thing that needs support and the best way to support it is to educate the patients and health care providers. AI has the potential to completely transform the delivery of health care, through better diagnostic outcomes, individualized treatment, as well as a more effective system. But all these can only be achieved provided that the stakeholders understand the possibilities and potential problems that may arise out of the system. From the patients' perspective, such education should be targeted at the explanation of what AI involves and what it offers to the healthcare system and patients. Some patients avoid using AI because of the complexity of the technology, or because they are worried about their privacy rights. These concerns can be solved by the clear and brief presentation of possible practical applications, for example, diagnostic gear based on artificial intelligence which is more effective in terms of early detection of diseases compared to existing methods. For example, in the diagnosis of pictures from radiological exams, AI algorithms can detect some irregularities that might not be seen by the human eye and the respective therapy can be started much faster (Dave & Patel, 2023). Likewise, AI based personalized medicine which prescribes and administers treatments according to patients' genetic makeup, habits and disease history, and has higher efficacy and fewer side effects. With these benefits spelled out clearly and backed by research, there is the possibility of trust and acceptation.

While consumers require information about AI for its proper use and utilization in a correct manner, the providers should undergo the process of enlightenment on the technicality of AI to allow it to be used appropriately and in the right manner. Training messages should focus on the fact that AI helps to save considerable time on administrative work, including appointments and paperwork so that clinicians could spend more time with patients. Through implementing AI to automate regular workloads, healthcare workers can increase the satisfaction of patients and quality of care. Furthermore, it is crucial for AI providers to know the shortcomings of the artificial intelligence system like bias coming from the training data set so that they will conform with the values of ethics on the use of the AI system. To achieve this learning, medical schools and every continuous professional development course should incorporate AI modules. It is also important that educational interventions should also meet the privacy and security concerns, which represents a core concept for both patients and providers. In a similar context to the points above, one can state that there is need to highlight the importance of secure encryption methods, anonymity/privacy, and compliance with the relevant legal Acts, such as HIPAA.

In order to establish trust in AI technologies, there is a need to establish a dialogue with patients and providers in order to show the possibility of using the technology as well as show the inherent risks of the technology. Committees and specific participants need to have a right to ask questions, get explanations and provide recommendations. For instance, one could organize a meeting in the form of an informative workshop or a webinar to ensure that both of these groups understand each other goals regarding AI implementation. Other patient education programs on how the AI is useful in attaining results shall engage and enable stakeholders to take an active part in the management of their health hence compliance with the prescribed therapies (Thorat et al., 2024).

Last of all, clearing misconceptions is a crucial step within the educational campaign. For instance, some people believe that, with AI being used in healthcare, it will soon supplant human Clinicians. Education should ensure that to healthcare providers, AI is not a rival for clinician wisdom but a supporter that can boost the quality and scope of care as well as its speed. This message also emphasizes on the need to have humans involved in any artificial intelligence health related process. This way, education becomes an integrated part of both patient care and provider training and the healthcare systems should promote an understanding of AI as a truthful partner. Therefore, stakeholders can learn from the experiences of experts and real-life application of AI to appreciate its possibilities hence enhancing effective implementation.

4.6.2 Ensuring Transparency and Accountability

Transparency and accountability are indispensable tools in building and sustaining trust, productive network, integrity and responsible leadership within governance systems, business entities, and in society at large. Transparency on the other hand involves the way organizations, governments and other entities conduct their affairs and availing of information those that are factual, accurate and current to parties interested in them. Accountability supports transparency by providing some form of punishment or winning the blame for some decision or other action. Combined these principles constitutes the fundamental good governance and organizational management principles. Transparency is the timely release of information concerning operations, choices and management systems. It helps the stakeholders to evaluate productivity of an organization and makes certain that the organization is operating within legal and ethical realm. For instance, in governance; transparency allow the citizens access to some of the governmental expenditure, policies and service delivery hence eliminating the gap between the state and the citizens. Likewise, in organizations, open communication on goals, issues and performance fastens employee confidence and stakeholder trust.

Whereas, Accountability prescribes ways and means of / evaluating and regulating organizational performance. This involves establishment of clear task, authority and responsibilities of the people and sub systems, in relation to organizational objectives and vision. It also calls for the availability of feedback mechanism, audits and evaluation mechanisms for measuring performance. For example, in corporate governance the accountability processes entail board monitoring, evaluations and compliance to the set of ethics. These measures serve at check and balances fraud, mismanagement, and inefficiencies in the operation. A Question of Trust notes that people trust accountability systems because they show that the reporting Organization has a strong commitment to ethical business practice. On balance of interests, it is crucial to determine the correlation between the transparency and accountability concepts as significant for the modern governance and the corporate world. Open systems make decision making understandable to the public and stakeholders while accountability makes leaders and institutions bear responsibility for their actions. Transparency of course is closely tied to accountability because while accountability is important it cannot work if it is not visible or seen and when there is no accountability then transparency becomes just an empty or symbolic gesture. For instance, in public-private partnership arrangements, the public has equal access to information on project delivery, while mechanisms like performance reviews to ensure delivery of the agreed upon obligations are met.

In workplaces, accountability means involving all key stakeholders and the general public in the exercise of power by reporting their activities. Managers require providing clear visions, reporting outcomes and soliciting feedback from the subordinates. Holding specific goals and responsibility for completing particular duties guarantee that employees take responsibility for their work. As a result of this duality on the part of both the leader and followers, there is less ambiguity, improved communication, and, thereby, increased levels of trust. It is not easy to maintain transparency and accountability especially in the large and complex organizations. A lack of access to critical data distorts transparency, as it only favors certain groups of people known as those with information asymmetry. Likewise, it may result to a scenario where accountability systems are also compromised and this results in the over exercise of power as well as corruption. To the above problems, solutions include sound legal frameworks, technology integration for operational monitoring, and ethical compliance. For example, in terms of transparency, the use of data in the form of a dashboard and blockchain can improve real-time information sharing, and improving the independence of the review boards. Finally, it is crucial to point out that transparency and accountability are crucial factors for good governance and ethical decision-making, as well as organizational performance. They establish an environment that fills the stakeholders with knowledge and power, and organizations discharge accountability and ethics. The implementation of these principles with reference to reliable systems and ethical management guarantees the sustainable and fair result of all the activities performed.

4.6.3 Long-Term Strategies for Trust-Building

This indicates that long term approach to trust development should be a critical consideration when seeking to create sustainable relationships and organizational success in the business, governance, health care and nonprofit sectors. Trust is the bedrock of any good partnerships and collaborations, as well as customer relations. In contrast to short-term approaches, tactics are long-term in their nature and stress the need for continuous, open, and sincere commitment to the building of trust on the part of the business over time. The most important of these is the need to be open in the transactional process that is going on. Transparency here entails the regular quality, breadth, depth, and frequency of communication with the stakeholders as to provide them with means for making rational decisions. When organizations or leaders share information on their goals, issues or performance with the public they are in effect telling people that they are truthful and accountable.

Another important aspect of trust management is the issue of accountability. To make trust to be effective there has to be an assurance of the responsibility of the individuals or organizations that are involved. Trust is a fragile thing and if people/organizations do not deliver as expected, then the trust is likely to disappear just as fast. Nevertheless, if they accept their authority and the blame for an error, and stand ready to change and do things right, trust can be rebuilt. In business and governance, matters of commitment can be addressed through audits, performance check as well as ensured by independent bodies. In personal relationships, too, people need to be held responsible for their actions in order to be dependable, and dependency is what is necessary to maintain trust. The philosopher John Rawls (2001) has touched on the question in A Theory of Justice when he stated that accountability was all about of getting things right for fairness and justice so that relationships could continue into the long-term.

The third way of building trust is by trying to show competence. It therefore follows that while trust is all about honesty and being open, a lot of it also depends on the capacity of an individual, or organization to fulfill their word. As the mentioned stakeholders observe the ability of the organization or leader to achieve what has been planned, and the problems solved, there will always be trust. This ought to be done through continued striving for the acquisition of the appropriate skills, working methods and techniques and structures that are necessary for achieving consistency. For instance, in customer relations, it will be evident that organizations that offer high quality customer goods and services over the years are likely to be trusted by their customers. Likewise, in the health care system earning the trust of the clients requires the health care provider to show that he or she is competent in clinical practice and that the clients always receive high quality services. In his book Trust and Reciprocity (2003) Gambetta states that competency communicates to others, an individual or an organisation, that they are trustworthy especially when the going gets tough. Another long-term strategy for trust building include sensitivity and empathy analysis within the working environment. Many people have found that the ability to communicate with the employees through emotional appeal usually leads to the employees giving their trust. Understanding of fellow human and ability to point the same to someone else also creates a bond that makes people value each other. In organizational context, empathy brings things like unity in groups, better commitments from employees, and better relationships between employers and employees. Empathy also used in management of conflict since it is easier to address the problems and find solution to them that will benefit both parties. According to Goleman (2006) in Emotional Intelligence, it worth to appreciate that emotions have critical functions of cultivating trust found in individual interpersonal relationships as well as at the organizational level.

Finally, establishing trust over time means that it needs to be done so consistently. The coherence of actions, behavior, and words provides credibility in the course of creating a strong foundation of trust. If leaders or organizations keep their word in the process or work according to what is expected of them, then trust is built. This means that the small things; that fill our daily lives, do count. Whether it is about ethical behavior, quality of services or delivery on promises, consistency gives stakeholders a predictable environment within which to interact with the organisation. As noted by Hosmer (1995) in Trust: The Common Thread between Organizational Theory and Philosophical Ethics, reliability is important in building trust because it cuts out uncertainty and provides assurance that individuals can rely on the actions of an organisation.

4.7 Ethical Frameworks for AI Development

Artificial Intelligence (AI) has grown tremendously and continues to so in the last few years bringing change in different fields for efficiency, innovation, and solution However, the potential of AI systems is enormous and a number of ethical questions arise because of this. From pre-empting biases in decision making algorithms to questions of ownership, privacy, transparency, and accountability AI development must reflect and conform to societal expectations. Ethical standards for artificial intelligence give AI the format and advice necessary to minimize such risks, ensure its fairness, and protect the general public's trust in AI systems.

1. **Foundational Principles of Ethical AI Development**

Ethical frameworks for AI development often draw from universally accepted principles of ethics and human rights. The foundational principles include:

- **Transparency**: AI application should be made in a way that can be easily communicated and controlled by the users and the stakeholders. By making decisions more transparent, there is an increased chance that the decision-making process by AI will be Supervised and checked by stakeholders.

- **Fairness**: AI systems cannot contain prejudice nor discrimination. It means that to guarantee that certain AI model will not reinforce historical biases, it needs to be trained on the reasonably diverse datasets and its performance needs to be constantly checked.

- **Accountability**: It is high time that developers and organizations owning the AI systems embraced themselves for the outcomes produced by their creations. This include developing ways on how much have been done in taking responsibility for the adversarial effects of AI and how else there conformities with AI ethical standards have been achieved.

- **Privacy**: Data privacy of users should be respected at all times. AI frameworks should address issues of how data is gathered and managed, and ensure user consent as well as meeting data privacy requirements such as GDPR.

- **Beneficence and Non-Maleficence**: An AI system should be one that will have the most benefits to individuals and society while in the same instance having the least effects of harm. It is important that developers should also avoid adding and exacerbating harm and that the AI system does not introduce new harm not seen at the outset.

These principles serve as a foundation for ethical frameworks but need to be contextualized for specific applications and industries.

2. **Key Ethical Frameworks for AI Development**

Many organizations, governments, as well as researchers have recommended the best strategies to follow in the creation of artificial intelligence. It can be noted that most of the frameworks are focused on the development of more or less similar AI systems that are responsible trustworthy, and aligned to human values.

a) **Asilomar AI Principles**

The Asilomar AI Principles: Ethiopia's contribution to the global conversation on how to guide AI into the future was adopted in 2017 by the Future of Life Institute. These principles focus on safety, openness, and how value is going to be created for all parties involved. Notable elements include:

- Ensuring AI safety through rigorous testing.

- Promoting shared prosperity by ensuring AI benefits are widely distributed.

- Upholding human values by ensuring that AI systems operate in ways that respect dignity, rights, and freedoms.

b) **OECD AI Principles**

The Organisation for Economic Co-operation and Development (OECD) adopted the set of principles for AI creation to build trust and development. These principles focus on five areas:

- AI should benefit people and the planet.

- AI systems should be fair and transparent.

- Robustness, security, and safety should be prioritized.

- Accountability should be ensured throughout the lifecycle of AI systems.

- Cross-border collaboration and international standards should guide AI governance.

c) European Union's Ethics Guidelines for Trustworthy AI

The European Union's guidelines emphasize "Trustworthy AI," which is defined by three main components:

- **Lawful**: Compliance with laws and regulations.

- **Ethical**: Adherence to ethical principles.

- **Robust**: Ensuring technical resilience to errors and vulnerabilities.

The framework also identifies seven requirements for trustworthy AI, including human agency, diversity, accountability, and privacy protection.

d) IEEE Ethically Aligned Design

The Institute of Electrical and Electronics Engineers (IEEE) has created a vast corpus called the Ethically Aligned Design. They focus on stakeholder engagement, environmentalism, and cultural relations. It promotes integration of ethical factors at the system design and development and deployment stages of AI.

3. Challenges in Implementing Ethical Frameworks

While ethical frameworks are essential, implementing them in practice is challenging. Common obstacles include:

- **Bias in AI Models**: Eliminating biases in datasets is a complex task, as data often reflects historical inequities. Developers must invest in ongoing audits and diverse data representation.

- **Lack of Accountability Mechanisms**: Determining accountability for AI-related harm can be challenging, especially when AI systems operate autonomously or when multiple stakeholders are involved.

- **Trade-offs Between Ethical Principles**: There are cases where principles such as privacy and transparency may be in variance. For instance, the steps to increase the transparency of AI might reveal trade secrets which can be disastrous to business.

- **Global Variability in Ethical Standards**: There are likewise varied points of view of the global community in terms of ethics in the use of AI. The following makes it challenging to develop theoretical structures that are useful in multiple countries.

4. The Role of Multi-Stakeholder Collaboration

Solving the problems considered within AI ethics is possible only through the cooperation of government bodies, business, educational institutions, and non-profit organizations. Removing this confusion is part of the governments' responsibility because they can pass laws that ensure the adherence to ethical AI while organizations can voluntarily adhere to guidelines and create internal ethics committee. The academics and the researchers act by fashioning techniques to identify and reduce ethical threats and the civil society to ensure that the public voices are well represented.

International collaborations like the Partnership on Artificial Intelligence and United Nations', AI for Good suggests, it's crucial to develop standards, which are universally acceptable to frame AI's ethical use.

5. Future Directions for Ethical AI Development

As AI technologies evolve, ethical frameworks must adapt to emerging challenges. For instance:

- The emergence of generative AI models needs new rules of intellectual property, fake news, and moderation.

- Latest technological innovations in autonomously controlled objects including self-driving automobiles require frameworks concerning safety, accountability or even ethical issues.

The combination of AI with quantum computing and bioengineering requires new ethical concerns about privacy, human enhancement, and threats to humanity.

Making research before a project is started and having an ongoing conversation with stakeholders, updating ethical frameworks more frequently, will be crucially important in addressing emerging challenges in AI development.

Ethical guidelines regulating the creation of AI systems are our best bet towards attaining and creating moral and objective AI systems that are also fair and reflect the society's values. These frameworks can maximize the value of AI for humanity if they provide a basis for the AI innovation consistent with such principles as transparency, accountability, and fairness. Although there are still some problems we are facing, cooperation and flexibility in approaching the solution will help to build a fair AI world.

4.7.1 International Guidelines for Responsible AI Use

Global standards for AI are important so that collectives of people, corporations and governments can implement them responsibly, securely and legally. Different stakeholders including, organizations and governments have also come up with guidelines of the use of AI in their practices in a bid to solve issues like unfairness, opaqueness, privacy and accountability among others. The OECD AI Principles is one of the first sets of international standards to address the issue of trustworthiness of AI. These principles require that AI reflects human rights and democratic values and demand that decision making by the AI should be transparent. They facilitative partnerships between governments, companies, and civil society so that the technology is positive and inclusive (OECD, 2019).

Also, in 2021 UNESCO provided detailed guidelines within the Recommendation on the Ethics of Artificial Intelligence. It emphasizes the need to protect human integrity, justice and backdrop. The guidelines highlight the idea of ethical aspects in the formation of AI, pointing out that human beings should control formation and work of artificial intelligence systems for the sake of keeping them useful and safe for society. Moreover, the recommendations of the European Commission relate to the appropriate application of generative AI, especially in research. These guidelines give recommendations on how to mitigate general risks of AI in the context of generative AI, so that its use would be ethical in research. Also, the ISO's 'standard on responsible AI ethics' correlates with the concept of fairness noting that great attention should be paid to the datasets which are used for AI training to avoid discrimination in AI approaches. It calls for the open account, with the implication that the AI systems should be understandable by the users. All together these guidelines set strong base of principles for ethical standard of using AI that will help to develop as well as deploy technologies across the world that will be beneficial to the society without posing threats or causing harm.

4.7.2 Principles of Fairness, Safety, and Transparency

The principles of fairness, safety, and transparency are essential in the area of Artificial Intelligence (AI) to speak about AI as the product that should be created and used in compliance with principles of ethics and human rights as well as to gain people's trust. AI fairness means lack of prejudice that may likely create discrimination to selected people or groups. I recently spoke to an employee who tragically shared she had been fired for 'being too emotional,' so I am very aware of how AI systems are trained on data and if this data has existing biases it will reinforce or even amplify them. Hence the need to make dataset as diverse as possible and do a rigorous check to make an AI algorithm as fairly endowing results as possible. There is also promoting the concept of fairness and this calls for balancing the operations done by the AI systems with the social, economic, cultural, and demographic factors involved in such decisions. The OECD guidelines and more recent ISO guidelines provide clear indications that fairness is a fundamental element to include in AI to achieve equal opportunities in decision making.

Safety is another very important principle that agrees with reducing potential negative impacts of the AI systems. This includes making sure that these new intelligent technologies are impervious to those cyber threats, that they are not a danger or harm to the body and mind. With the growing application of the AI systems, the safety is paramount in sensitive areas like health, transport and business. Accountable AI frameworks place a strong focus on the fact that safety concerns should be integrated into AI creation and deployment mechanisms, at the design stage as well as afterward, with processes for monitoring and updating in place to counteract emergent adverse effects. Transparency with regards to AI means that the AI systems are explainable, traceable, and observable. The general public and other stakeholders should be able to understand the reasoning of such systems and other factors that might have a bearing on their decision making. With the help of the following principle, the primary goal is to ensure that people trust AI: this means that actions must be explained properly where they are needed most, for example, when determining employment opportunities or guilt in a criminal case. This is importance because the errors as well as bias into the system, can be detected and looked into depending on the level of transparency provided by the AI system to enable accountability in the process of arriving at the decision that leads to a particular action by the AI system. As AI advanced in various sectors, transparency make sure that AI's implementation is accountable and fair. Combined, these principles form a framework to the appropriate deployment of AI, so that these technologies foster the common good and avoid causing harm and injustice.

4.7.3 Promoting Multi-Stakeholder Collaboration

Dedication to the development and implementation of AI Multimedia requires collaboration from diverse stakeholders who can support the creation of positive change, avoiding negative advancement of technology. AI development is associated with the various intricate problems, and they include the ethical issues, legal issues and social issues. Evidently, this means that multi-stakeholder cooperation, including governments, businesses, civil society, academia, and international organizations, is essential for policy, framework, and best practice determining the direction of AI development. With focus on the multi-stakeholder collaboration it is crucial to identify the advantage of connecting the technical knowledge with the requirement of the society. Although developers and engineers working on AI technologies and systems may pay most of their attention to the technological impacts, other stakes may contribute to the understanding of social, ethical, and legal aspects of the applications of AI. For example, the government should ensure that AI is implemented in a way that is most beneficial and supportive of the government's plans and policies to meet societal needs while NGOs should make efforts to ensure that the AI is in the best interest of minorities, and AI does not discriminate against individuals of color or any nationality.

In addition, it is appreciated that stakeholders with different backgrounds can warn about potential risks associated with the AI use, including algorithmic bias, security issues, and detrimental side effects. This paper concludes that inclusive AI governance enables improved public trust in decisions made due to the inclusion of the various sectors. Another benefit of developing AI strategy by engaging multiple stakeholders is that it becomes easier to create international guidelines for the effective use of AI by implementing policies that give everyone a fair chance to achieve success while using it safely, and transparently. Engagement of the global society is central to AI management. This is underlined by the decision-making model which the multi-stakeholder framework copied from internet governance. This model ensures that the gains arising out of AI are enjoyed by many and that everyone will come together to resolve the issues arising from the use of AI at the international level for development that respects human rights and the general welfare of humanity.

CHAPTER 5

The Future of AI and Big Data in Healthcare

5.1 Emerging Trends in AI Technologies

AI is undergoing a transformative evolution which is redefining the way in which things are done in healthcare, education, transportation, and so much more. The increasing sophistication and applicability of AI systems to emerging trends in AI technologies suggests that AI systems are becoming more human-like, more capable with decision making and more automated. The combination of AI with the cutting edge of methodologies heralds a new era of problem solving and innovation in all industries.

1. **The Rise of Generative AI Models**

   Generating text, images and videos has been one of the biggest breakthroughs in AI, and generative models like Generative Pre-trained Transformers (GPTs) or Diffusion Models take it further by allowing computers to create data content. Based on deep learning frameworks, these systems use a lot of analysis of very big datasets and can even create content similar to human creativity. Created by generating realistic outputs with minimal human intervention, generative AI is revolutionizing content creation, customer service and education (Rane et al., 2024).

2. **Hybrid AI: Bridging Symbolic Reasoning and Machine Learning**

   However, the symbolic reasoning and machine learning combined in hybrid AI models is much more capable to generate better contextual understanding, and then make logical decisions. Traditional machine learning aims at pattern recognition by data driven means, while symbolic reasoning has logic and knowledge representation.

Complementing these methods, integration of these methods yields tolerant solutions to complex problems in natural language understanding and healthcare diagnostics (Shuford & Islam, 2024).

3. **Intelligent Automation and Process Optimization**

Industry is leaning toward automating complex tasks with AI; in the process of making the most of efficiency and limiting operational costs. Intelligent Process Automation (IPA) applies AI technologies, at the intersection of RPA, NLP, and computer vision, to automate workflows. This allows businesses to reallocate resources from repetitious, manual processes, to innovation and strategic initiatives.

4. **AI for Personalization and User-Centric Design**

Personalized AI solutions are transforming consumer interactions across digital platforms. Recommender systems, voice assistants, and adaptive learning platforms employ AI to cater to individual user preferences and needs. For instance, e-commerce platforms use AI algorithms to analyze customer behavior and recommend products, while educational technologies adapt content delivery based on students' learning styles. This trend underscores the importance of user-centric AI in enhancing engagement and satisfaction.

5. **Ethical AI and Explain ability**

The growing deployment of AI systems has brought ethical considerations to the forefront. Ensuring fairness, accountability, and transparency in AI algorithms is a critical challenge. Explainable AI (XAI) seeks to address these issues by making AI decisions interpretable and understandable to humans. This is particularly important in high-stakes applications such as criminal justice, healthcare, and finance, where opaque decision-making processes could lead to significant societal harm (Dwivedi et al., 2023).

6. **Edge AI and Decentralized Computing**

Edge AI represents a shift toward decentralized computation, enabling AI processing to occur directly on devices rather than relying solely on cloud infrastructure. This reduces latency, improves privacy, and allows for real-time decision-making. Edge AI applications are particularly valuable in Internet of Things (IoT) ecosystems, where devices like sensors and wearables can process data locally for faster and more efficient operations (Kim et al., 2023).

7. AI Integration with Big Data and IoT

The convergence of AI with Big Data and IoT technologies is paving the way for smarter systems capable of analyzing massive datasets in real-time. This integration allows for enhanced predictive analytics, anomaly detection, and decision-making across industries. For instance, smart cities utilize AI-driven insights to optimize traffic flow, reduce energy consumption, and improve public safety.

8. AI in Autonomous Systems

The development of autonomous systems, such as self-driving cars and drones, showcases the potential of AI to navigate complex environments. These systems rely on a combination of machine learning, computer vision, and sensor fusion to interpret surroundings and make decisions. Advances in autonomous technologies are expected to transform industries such as transportation, logistics, and defense.

9. Advancements in Natural Language Processing (NLP)

NLP continues to be a prominent area of AI research, with advancements in contextual understanding, sentiment analysis, and conversational AI. Pre-trained models such as BERT (Bidirectional Encoder Representations from Transformers) and GPT are pushing the boundaries of what machines can achieve in language comprehension and generation. These technologies are being applied in virtual assistants, chatbots, and automated content moderation.

10. Future Research Directions in AI

Emerging trends indicate that future research in AI will focus on developing more robust, scalable, and human-centric systems. Efforts are underway to address challenges related to bias, scalability, and generalization. Researchers are also exploring interdisciplinary approaches, combining AI with neuroscience, biology, and physics, to unlock novel applications.

In conclusion, emerging trends in AI technologies highlight the rapid evolution of intelligent systems across various domains. From generative models to edge computing and ethical AI, these advancements promise to reshape industries and enhance the quality of human life. However, addressing ethical challenges and ensuring the equitable distribution of AI benefits will remain critical for its sustainable growth.

5.2 Next-Generation Smart Healthcare Systems

Cyber-physical systems, the Internet of Things (IoT), cloud computing, artificial intelligence, and blockchain are the defining components of the forthcoming industrial revolution, referred to as Industry 4.0. The Internet of Things (IoT) seeks to facilitate the seamless integration of diverse smart devices, hence enabling the amalgamation of numerous sensors, computational resources, and actuators. Sensors provide the awareness of the external world, while actuators enable the system to deliver a physical response to users. These sensors and actuators are utilised in several applications, including healthcare, transportation, and surveillance, among others. Cloud computing offers computational resources for the distant execution of various activities and delivers results to several applications. The emerging concepts of Artificial Intelligence (AI) and Machine Learning (ML) provide customers superior services, minimal response times, scalability, and resilience to diverse user requirements. The requirements of healthcare applications have escalated due to contemporary AI applications being data-intensive. Furthermore, the contemporary volume of patients, varieties of analyses, and reaction time demands are becoming stringent. Novel illnesses are identified daily; innovative treatments must undergo testing through simulations, and, crucially, healthcare apps must be implemented utilising resilient and scalable frameworks that deliver high-quality outcomes in little time.

The challenge of delivering universal healthcare is attributed to three primary factors. Primarily, the majority of patients require constant monitoring and real-time data analysis. This is a challenge because to the vastness of the data, necessitating substantial processing resources and effective methods. Furthermore, the high expense of substantial computational power renders the accessibility of healthcare for all individuals the second most significant obstacle. The third challenge is maintaining integrity and reliability of systems. Healthcare data is very sensitive as it may be exploited by terrorists or pharmaceutical monopolists to target certain populations. This necessitates frameworks that are tamper-proof and secure against hacking, hence avoiding any fraudulent alteration of critical healthcare data. The subsequent approach is advised to consolidate the technologies emblematic of the Industry 4.0

revolution, hence providing a comprehensive end-to-end integrated solution for healthcare.

- **IoT paradigm**

  The IoT paradigm consists of various IoT devices equipped with corresponding healthcare sensors and actuators. Common healthcare sensors within the IoT framework encompass blood pressure sensors, pulse oximeters, electrocardiograms, body temperature sensors, and airflow sensors. These sensors are geographically dispersed and monitor the external environment to facilitate decision-making and provide utilities for the respective system. The devices are fundamentally energy-limited and execute modest computing functions, although potentially producing substantial data in a brief timeframe. Consequently, to analyse IoT data and facilitate pertinent applications, intelligent systems utilise advanced deep learning models, including Convolutional Neural Networks (CNNs) and sequence models such as Long Short-Term Memory (LSTM) networks. The approach further provides infrastructure, platform, and software services for Edge and Cloud computing. The perceived data signals and functional needs, including anticipated accuracy rate, data sensing frequency, and service delivery deadlines, are transmitted to computing paradigms inside the IoT realm.

- **Gateway Level**

  Gateway-level devices encompass cellphones and mobile computers, such as laptops and tablets, serving as an interface between the IoT layer and computing resources. These devices aggregate data and organise it into tasks for transmission to the IoT-Fog broker. These devices can be configured to manage data, albeit to a limited degree, in accordance with user standards or application Quality of Service (QoS) characteristics. Developing software modules for these devices is complex, as a single gateway device may link to several IoT devices or sensors, necessitating the management of data and service demands for each sensor or user. Moreover, these devices are susceptible to various security risks and malicious attacks that might compromise data or disrupt one or more of these gateway devices. Various solutions may be employed to alleviate these challenges, such as virtualisation, encryption, and blockchain-based data management, facilitating enhanced and smooth communication across IoT devices, gateway nodes, and broker nodes through close contact with broker and worker nodes.

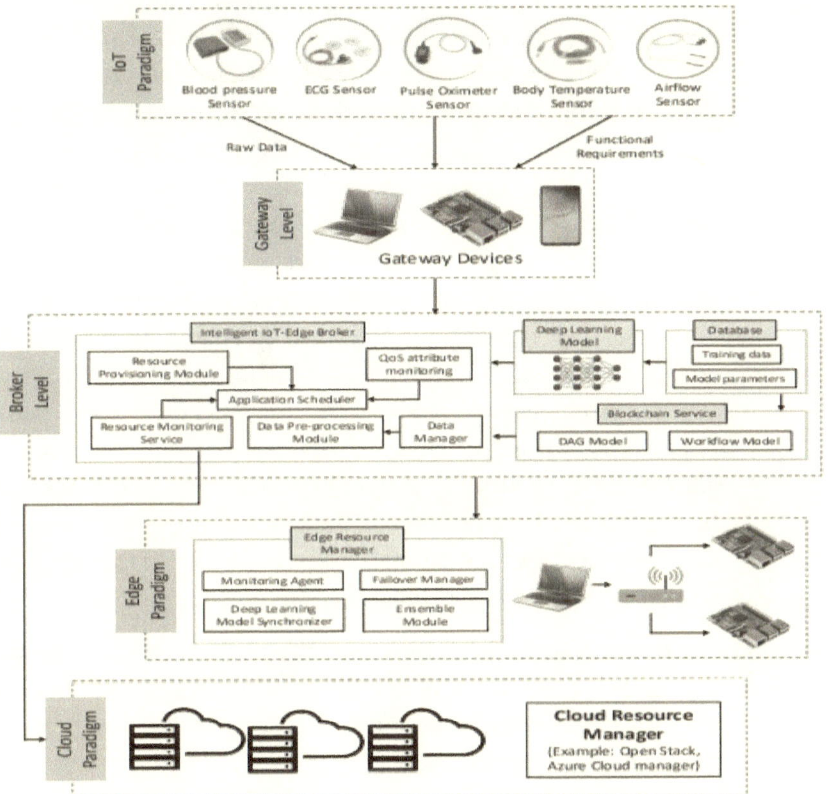

Figure 5.1: Model leveraging advanced technologies of Artificial Intelligence and Blockchain for enhanced performance and seamless task execution on Fog computing Environments.

Source: - (Tuli et al., 2020)

- **Broker Level**

  1. **IoT-Edge Broker (IEB)-** This is implemented at the broker level and serves as the fundamental component of the model that mediates and makes critical choices for the computational network. It comprises a collection of sub-components with distinct purposes. Functioning as an intermediary between the IoT and Edge computing paradigms, it is tasked with comprehending the context of IoT devices and application scenarios, overseeing

the performance of Edge nodes, facilitating resource discovery, strategizing for preemptive resource configuration before application deployment, dynamically provisioning resources, and managing the execution of IoT applications to fulfil their QoS requirements while addressing framework faults. Within IEB, the Data Manager oversees interactions between the gateway node and IoT devices, while the QoS Attribute Monitor evaluates the IoT context and the status of the Edge infrastructure, forecasts demand, tracks the fulfilment of QoS attributes, assesses the characteristics of Edge and Cloud nodes via the Resource Monitoring Service, and enables application placement with fault tolerance through the Resource Provisioning Module. The Application Scheduler implements policies and methodologies to sustain system performance by assigning tasks to the most suitable Edge or Cloud nodes, ensuring optimal Quality of Service and adherence to application deadlines using predictive models and heuristics. The Data Pre-processing Module filters and transforms data into the necessary formats and transmits it to the designated worker node, which may be located in the Edge or Cloud.

2. **Deep Learning Models**- These are stored in a communal repository and work as dynamic learning models that adjust to the performance measurements or loss functions established by developers to meet user needs and application performance. The model's accessibility presents concerns, such as potential cyberattacks from hackers who may either take the model or intentionally alter it, therefore diminishing its accuracy or predictive performance. A further problem is ensuring the confidentiality of the training data while permitting all users to access and utilize the deep learning models without intricate authentication systems. Diverse differential privacy training models may be employed, and the training and cross-validation datasets can be securely encrypted in a protected database.

3. **Database**- The Database, situated at the gateway level or higher depending on resource availability, serves as a register for preserving instance sensor data and metadata related to applications and data flows, while IEB utilizes its services for resource discovery. The database further retains the parameters of the deep learning model and the training data in an

encrypted manner. The model weights and biases are dynamically stored on distributed blockchains to ensure integrity and reliable execution and prediction of input data.

4. **Blockchain Service-** This service preserves the integrity of the sensor data and model parameters. Various services and strategies are available to achieve the same objective, each with distinct access speeds and overhead characteristics. Trade-offs must be meticulously evaluated to ensure that reaction speed and data integrity remain uncompromised. In Big Data contexts, it is essential to carefully allocate Edge or Cloud nodes for hashing, mining, and proof-of-work computations, taking into account resource limitations and the dependability of edge devices.

- **Infrastructure Level**

Edge and Cloud Infrastructures consist of virtualized resources such as virtual machines and containers, provided via centralised data centers and distributed Edge nodes. Edge and Cloud Infrastructures both own distinct resource managers: The Edge Resource Manager (ERM) and the Cloud Resource Manager (CRM). They are tasked with (1) assessing the condition of the relevant infrastructure, (2) forecasting performance, (3) resource virtualisation (virtual machines and containers), (4) pooling, (5) scaling, (6) coordinating, and (7) optimisation (migration and consolidation). Furthermore, they provide service redundancy and dependability in supporting the IEB to guarantee fault tolerance during unpredictable occurrences like as node failures, resource outages, and security breaches. They periodically synchronize the parameters of the deep learning model and maintain majority consensus for data blocks inside the blockchain network to uphold uniform deep learning models and sensor data. The proposed model's use cases encompass a data marketplace for personal information, enabling users to selectively sell their data to healthcare providers and insurance companies, while prioritizing user consent, facilitated by blockchain-based data provenance tracking. The three foundational elements of next-generation technologies—Artificial Intelligence, Blockchain, and IoT—facilitate the development of solutions addressing challenges related to accuracy, device calibration, and the enhancement of data security and privacy.

5.2.1 Designing AI-Driven Smart Hospitals

Smart hospitals driven by AI therefore involves the integration of AI, the Internet of Things (IoT), big data analytics, and cloud computing in order to design the hospital in which the nurse is automated through technologies. AI is used by these hospitals to improve clinical decision making, streamline operations and personalize patient care while still making healthcare as efficient and patient cantered as possible. Predictive analytics, intelligent resource management, and the seamless integration of an interconnected system of systems, all of which are able to generate real time data to inform decisions, are some key elements that make up smart hospital design. The main application of AI technologies in smart hospitals is predictive analytics — early detection of diseases and improving diagnostics. In use, Machine learning algorithms swallow enormous datasets and bring out patterns that help predict how a patient will fare and prescribe a treatment plan specific to each patient. An example would be that AI integrated with IoT device to monitor patient vitals in real time and alert for immediate intervention when any anomaly is detected which is helping to reduce response times and save patients safety (Subash Chandra Nayak, 2024).

Additionally, smart hospitals use big data analytics to help them to optimize resource allocation and operational workflow. These systems use historical and real time data to predict patient admissions, bed occupancy and staff scheduling. This fuels the process of cloud computing that lets healthcare providers seamlessly access patient records and medical reports between departments, so that healthcare professionals can collaborate well as well as take decision based on data. The integration increase productivity and decrease burden for administrative activities (Talib et al., 2023).

Beyond operational efficiency, smart hospital design also takes into account a personalized care brought by AI driven tools. Natural language processing (NLP) powered chatbots and virtual assistants improve patient engagement and satisfaction by allowing patients to interact with health information and to schedule appointments virtually. Consistent with that, wearable devices and remote monitoring systems have the potential of continuous health tracking that allows patients to manage their chronic condition from home while decreasing hospital readmissions. The design of AI driven smart hospitals is also guided by ethical considerations. Trust in AI systems depends on transparency, security of the data and the patient consent. Healthcare solutions using advanced technologies must be built robustly giving equal consideration to data privacy concerns. Therefore design of AI driven smart hospitals require a multidisciplinary approach that encompasses technological innovation, ethical practices and patient centric care to build resilient systems of care (Mirbabaie et al., 2022).

Finally, AI driven smart hospitals are a paradigmatic shift in global healthcare based on technology that allows delivering superior patient outcomes and streamlined operations along with patient specific care. Research into these systems will need to continue to address the challenges and to bring about the ideal realization of the potential of smart hospital innovations as these systems evolve.

5.2.2 Predictive Maintenance for Medical Equipment

An advanced approach to medical equipment maintenance, commonly referred to as Predictive Maintenance (Pd.M.) is the use of data analytics, machine learning (ML), and IoT to predict an equipment failure before it happens. Such an approach greatly improves the efficiency of the healthcare by guaranteeing medical devices remain working and reliable, reducing unplanned down times, and improving patient outcomes. It involves using real time data, historical performance metric, and predictive algorithms to identify the condition of the equipment, intervene timely and reduce the requirement of reactive repairs (Manchadi et al., 2023). In healthcare, Pd.M. is a core component that involves the use of IoT enabled sensors, that continuously monitor critical parameters such as temperature, vibration, and usage pattern. Data from these sensors are sent back to centralized systems and ML models analyze patters, detect anomalies, and predict impending failures. For example, research demonstrates that such systems can forecast near future failures in, for example, imaging devices like MRI and CT scanners and lead to reduced service interruptions as well as efficient planning of maintenance tasks (Shamayleh et al., 2020). This approach not only stretches the lifespan of the equipment but also its operational safety.

In addition, Pd.M. also improves cost efficiency in healthcare implementation. Hospitals thus avoid sudden breakdowns, reduce repair costs, optimize inventory management of spare parts, and generally increase the utilization of all assets. Additionally, predictive models facilitate the transition of maintenance from time based to condition based in which maintenance schedules are specific to the actual performance and wear of the equipment. More sustainable operations are enabled by this flexibility especially in resource constrained facilities. Pd.M. has an important mechanism to facilitate compliance, patient safety, etc. St DE medical devices, especially those used in the critical care and diagnostics, must be safe. Pd.M. guarantees these devices are operating as intended in order to reduce the risks of mis made diagnoses or delayed treatments. According to studies, predictive maintenance reduces emergency downtime by up to 30% and improves operational availability by 20%, however, the benefits of predictive maintenance directly affect clinical workflows and patient care outcomes.

Yet, there are many challenges in the adoption of Pd.M.; this includes high costs of implementation, integration of data, and people with skill. However, the ongoing AI and data analytics advancements are inspiring healthcare to embrace the Pd.M. concept as a core for practicing modern medical equipment management.

5.2.3 Integrated Systems for Seamless Care Delivery

In the current healthcare world, integrated systems for seamless care delivery are fundamental in delivering cohesive, patient cantered services in various levels of care settings. Such systems aim to break down barriers that exist within a broken healthcare structure using technology to coordinate care, aligning workflows and improving communication between providers. Seamless care delivery is the essence of care delivery with a continuum of care meant that the patients have documented care transitions between various healthcare services ranging from primary care to specialized treatment, rehabilitation and community based support (Parnaby & Towill, 2008). It is because the foundation of integrated healthcare systems is interprofessional collaboration, sharing of data infrastructure, and smoother care pathways. For example, studies indicate that healthcare networks integration will lead to better patient outcomes by enabling care providers from various fields of professional practice to work cohesively, without duplicating services and increasing efficiency (van Wijngaarden et al., 2006). For example, medical clinics linked to pharmacy services reduce patient harm due to better medical adherence and adverse drug reactions for best patient safety and health outcomes.

Electronic health records (EHRs) along with interoperable health IT systems are technology critical enablers for seamless care delivery. On the other hand, EHRs make it possible for providers to obtain comprehensive patient information in real time that will enable them to make informed decisions, and will reduce delays in treatment. An expanded telemedicine and sometimes, digital health platform has also increased access to care and bridged gaps in the delivery of healthcare services, particularly for the 'under served' populations (Strandberg-Larsen & Krasnik, 2009). These tools improve communication between patients and providers and keep care moving forward, regardless of location. Patient engagement and empowerment is also a core part of the emphasis made in integrated systems. Technology, along with shared decision-making models and collaborative structures for care, offer patients and caregivers opportunities to contribute toward development of personalized care plans (Wojtak et al., 2019)there is growing recognition that we need to transform education and training to support clinical professionals, managers and leaders to work in new ways. Delivering care in an integrated system requires different competencies and skills at every positional level in order to support more collaborative and seamless care for patients. Traditional leadership and clinical training programs are insufficient to meet the needs of integrated care delivery and as a result, many educational institutions and training programs are looking to address this as a critical gap. In fall 2018, IFIC launched a new Special Interest Group (SIG. These approaches are related to better adherence to medical treatment protocols and greater satisfaction with the way medical care is delivered.

Although integrated systems may offer great benefits, implementing such systems to deliver seamless care is by no means easy. Three barriers to technology integration are organizational resistance, data privacy concerns, and lack of standardization in technology integration. In addition, there is substantial investment in training healthcare professionals to transition into new working and collaborative practices. Several frameworks and metrics have been developed in order to measure the effectiveness of these systems. Continuity of care, patient satisfaction, cost-efficiency and health outcomes are these. These are evaluations that are needed to close the gaps in the system as well as optimize the integrated systems. Therefore, integrated systems for care delivery without seams are a transformative approach to modern healthcare. These systems, which foster collaboration, and use technology, as well as patient cantered practices, tackle the inherent complexity of healthcare delivery in a way that has a dramatic impact on improving care quality and efficiency. To achieve full realization of seamless care delivery we must continue research and innovation to overcome existing challenges.

5.3 Empowering Patients Through AI

Artificial Intelligence (AI) is a disruptive way to empower patients to redefine how healthcare is delivered, involve patients in their care and provide personalized care. AI driven technologies, like machine learning algorithms, generative AI as well as predictive analytics serve to give patients more autonomy in handling their health and permitting access to specific, tailored healthcare alternatives. These have changed care of the patients to more proactive, specific, and equitable. Personalized healthcare made possible by AI is one of the biggest ways AI makes patients more empowered. Algorithms use personal patient data to make personalized treatment recommendation. AI empowered systems capture heterogeneous data, including gene, medical history and lifestyle factor to infer future health risks and suggest prevention measures. As an example, generative AI has demonstrated potential to tailor medical interventions to the particular needs of individual patients using the wealth of information available in the healthcare datasets (Selvaraj, 2024). Customized approaches not only boost treatment efficiency but also help patients by giving them the power of what is known as actionable health insights.

AI also helps patients stay connected to their healthcare providers, through real time communication. Today, many context aware and personalized health information are delivered to consumers through AI powered chatbots and virtual assistants. For example, during the COVID-19 pandemic, AI driven chatbots were instrumental in helping to disseminate accurate, timely information to older adults helping them make informed decisions about their health (X. Wang et al., 2021). In addition to improving health literacy, such tools can reduce the need for patients to visit physical consultations for routine queries and thereby keep both patients and providers more time.

Additionally, wearable devices paired with AI algorithms have been empowering patients with continuous health monitoring, and giving early warnings about possible health issue. They are these devices that collect real time data of vital parameters like heart rate, blood pressure and blood glucose levels and analyses the same using AI to find abnormalities and predict adverse events. These technologies enable patients to take control over their wellness and contribute positively to better health outcome by allowing patients to monitor their health and to act when appropriate. On the other hand, AI democratizes access to health care by tackling widening resource gaps and also increasing outreach to the underserved. AI powered telemedicine platforms have closed the urban rural divide of healthcare services by expanding healthcare access to remote and rural areas. For example, AI based diagnostic tools can be used to high accuracy on medical images, so that that primary care providers in a low resource setting can offer advanced diagnostic services without the need for specialist input.

Moreover, AI facilitates patient care with shared decision-making, giving clear evidence-based insights for patients and health care providers to work together to make treatment decisions. AI fuelled decision support systems use clinical guidelines and patient specific data to integrate for recommendations improving the quality of clinical decisions. Not only does it empower patients but it also inherently builds trust into healthcare systems by guaranteeing that treatment decisions are made after having considered adequate (and patient's preferred) information (Koutsouleris et al., 2022)we explore the promises and challenges of artificial intelligence (AI. There are challenges with the use of AI for patient empowerment, but its potential is there. Major barriers are related to data privacy, algorithmic biases, the digital divide. To achieve equitable access to AI tools, these challenges need to be addressed through robust regulation behind which there are inclusive design principles. Such as AI systems need to be trained on different datasets in order to prevent bias and achieve equally good results for all patient populations. In conclusion, AI has revolutionised healthcare by providing personalised treatment, real-time health monitoring, and improved engagement tools. These advances allow people to better manage their health, improve results, and gain greater control. To empower patients and achieve equal healthcare access, AI must solve its problems as it evolves.

5.3.1 Wearable Devices and Personalized Health Apps

Wearable devices & personalized health application is a game changing advancement in modern healthcare, where technology and medicine harmoniously join together to facilitate continuous monitoring, preventive care as well as personalized treatment methods. This has made these tools popular because they can be used to collect real time health data, engage patients and help healthcare providers take action. Wearables and health apps based on biosensors and mobile platforms are instrumental to reshaping how healthcare services are delivered and managed, and the effect on patient outcomes, while offloading the stress on existing healthcare systems.

To measure physiological parameters continuously, wearable devices, such as smartwatches, fitness trackers and medical grade biosensors, are designed. Such devices rely on recent advanced technology to measure metrics like heart rate, oxygen saturation, physical activity and sleep patterns, etc. Wearable technology has proven particularly useful in real time disease monitoring of chronic diseases like diabetes, cardiovascular conditions, and hypertension. For the case of diabetes, continuous glucose monitors (CGMs) facilitate exchange of glucose levels in real time, to assist with adjustments in medication or lifestyle interventions (Guk et al., 2019). Likewise, among the diseases for which Bluetooth-compatible health wearables such as Bluetooth sensors have improved the management considerably are cardiovascular diseases with early detection and intervention made possible through the right tools (Canali et al., 2022)as tools for biomedical research and clinical care. In this context, wearables are considered key tools for a more digital, personalised, preventive medicine. At the same time, wearables have also been associated with issues and risks, such as those connected to privacy and data sharing. Yet, discussions in the literature have mostly focused on either technical or ethical considerations, framing these as largely separate areas of discussion, and the contribution of wearables to the collection, development, application of biomedical knowledge has only partially been discussed. To fill in these gaps, in this article we provide an epistemic (knowledge-related.

Personalized health apps and wearable devices further amplify their utility in that they can be further integrated into wearable devices to provide platforms for data analysis, goal setting and behaviour modification. Wearables collect data and algorithms within health apps analyze that data to offer actionable recommendations and insights specific to the user's health profile. For instance, applications can tell users when their heart rhythm is irregular, when the best times for physical activity tied to their sleep cycle might be, or advise on dietary changes to improve metabolic health. The personalized approach is consistent with the larger field of precision medicine, whereby healthcare interventions are made based on individual genetic, environmental and lifestyle factors.

Wearable devices and health apps have one of the most important contributions in preventive healthcare. Continuous monitoring of these key health metrics allows these tools to help individuals identify potential health problems before they become worse. Wearable biosensors that measure stress levels or sleep quality can aid users in understanding stress and fatigue related disorders or ways in which they can help to promote mental health. As with fitness trackers, they encourage physical activity and healthier lifestyles by setting customizable goals and providing feedback on how close or removed you are from your goal, which greatly diminishes the risks of obesity, cardiovascular disease, and many other lifestyle related conditions (García-Magariño et al., 2019).

Additionally, wearable technology and health apps are also being used in clinical research and patient tailored treatment. These tools are used by researchers and clinicians to collect granular and ongoing data over long periods to identify fine details and correlations that might not be seen as part of standard point in time assessments. For instance, wearable devices used in the clinics for neurodegenerative diseases (e.g., gait, balance or fine motor skills) can inform on the disease progression and treatment efficacy. Furthermore, these technologies provide remote monitoring; the reduction in healthcare expenses and makes healthcare more accessible by monitoring chronic illnesses and post-surgical treatment through the absence of frequent in person visits.

While numerous benefits are associated with wearable devices and health apps, they have difficulties that impede their widespread adoption and efficient functionality. The accuracy and reliability of data is one of the biggest issues. In recent years, wearables have improved very much, but also data accuracy can vary depending on the quality of the sensors, environmental conditions and user compliance. For example, motion artifacts may confuse these as heart rate changes linking to erroneous conclusions. Also, data integration from many devices and platforms present interoperability problems since not all platforms and devices use similar protocols for sharing and analysing data.

Adoption is also hampered by a number of privacy and security concerns. The wearable & app applications generating vast amounts of sensitive health data give rise to concerns about data breaches, unauthorized access and misuse. To gain trust of their users, it is crucial ensuring robust encryption, compliance with data protection regulations as well as transparency of privacy policies. In addition, there is a requirement for well specified and regulatory mechanisms that monitor the development and deployment of wearable health technologies such that they fully comply with accepted requirements pertaining to safety, efficacy and ethical use.

Beyond those technical and regulatory barriers, disparities in the access and digital literacy barrier also prevent the equitable provision of the benefits wearable technologies and health apps offer. These devices perpetuate existing health inequities if the people in underserved or low-income communities do not have the resources or knowledge to use the devices using effectively. To fill these gaps, it is necessary to reduce the cost and device usability of wearable devices, and to train people digitally health literate across varied populations. In the future, wearable devices and personalized health apps are poised to shine, with artificial intelligence (AI), machine learning (ML) and data analytics all poised to make them better and better. With AI powered algorithms, you can have more sophisticated interpretations of health data, generating predictive insights and recommended with higher accuracy. To provide one example, wearable data based predictive models could tell users about potential health risks, say cardiovascular events or exacerbations of chronic conditions, days in advance. In addition, wearables linked to other digital health technologies, notably telemedicine platforms and electronic health records, can afford a smooth pathway from field to the patient and eliminates fragmentation between care, which leads to increased coordination of care and better patient outcomes.

In this manner wearable devices and personalized health apps have changed the way healthcare is delivered and experienced, from reactive to proactive care. Empowering people with real time insights and personalised recommendations enable healthier lifestyles, better disease management and support for preventive interventions. But accuracy, privacy, accessibility, and even interoperability challenges hinder their full deployment. Advancements in technology continue and the overcoming these barriers are an important part of what is to come in the future of healthcare with wearable health technologies poised to be a mainstay in the healthcare experience of the future with a more connected, more efficient, more patient centric experience.

5.3.2 Democratizing Health Information with AI Tools

Cyber ethics is the underpinning of the ethical aspects of SDM which refers to take an ethical stand when dealing with patient autonomy and beneficence. SDM promotes the principle of informed consent because it ensures patient's full information on risks, benefits and uncertainties of their care. In furtherance, it is consistent with the larger goals of patient cantered care which focus on individual wellbeing and dignity. There are important ethical challenges to face including how to deal with when patients' preferences diverge from evidence-based recommendations. As clinicians, they strive to strike the balance between respect for the patient's autonomy, the need to engage with patient in transparent and empathetic way.

Finally, shared decision making is an important element of modern patient cantered care, one in which the patient and provider work together in partnership, with trust, and with mutual respect. But its benefits are not only related to better health outcomes, they include more empowered and satisfied patients. Yet realizing the full potential of SDM requires overcoming barriers tied to time, health literacy and the power dynamics between the patient and providers; and, new technological innovations which improve accessibility and efficiency. In healthcare systems, SDM will be essential to delivering personalized, equitable and high-quality care as healthcare systems evolve.

Wearable health devices paired with AI algorithms are the most important part in democratizing health information by continuously monitoring vital parameters like heart rate, blood pressure and glucose levels. These devices go beyond individuals tracking their health metrics to real time-sharing data with healthcare providers for making better informed medical decisions (Salam & N, 2024). One example is when an AI powered wearable helps individuals with chronic diseases, like diabetes or hypertension, know of changes in their health status early on to gain timely medical intervention. Furthermore, these tools strengthen patients and providers' collaborative relationship, and the patients are encouraged to make shared decision over and personalized care.

Health information is also distributed differently than it was before, with the removal of barriers of literacy and language through the use of AI. Using natural language processing (NLP) capabilities, AI systems can provide medical information in more user-friendly format, converting complex terminology to understandable language for the inexperienced. Moreover, AI tools provide multilingual support, inclusive of various populations with different languages, and such absence of communication barriers (A. Chen et al., 2024). By providing easier avenues to real health information these systems free people to make better decisions regarding their health without fear of misinformation or gross neglect of care.

Using AI tools in health education makes health education even more democratic in the sense that it offers personalised learning experiences of patients and healthcare professionals. For example, the virtual platforms with the help of AI powered interactive modules and simulations can make individuals aware of medical condition, and their treatment options. In addition, these platforms keep health care providers in tune about the latest development in medical science for continuous professional development (Bedington et al., 2024). This leads to health literacy across all stakeholders in the healthcare ecosystem, and to closing the knowledge gap between one and the other.

However, despite these benefits, both the ethical considerations and governance challenges inherent in AI for democratizing health information must be overcome for full realization of AI's promise. The number of issues related to data privacy, algorithmic bias and equitable access, require strong regulatory frameworks and stakeholder collaboration. Building trust with users requires also the security of patient data and transparency in AI decision making processes. For that, efforts to eliminate the bias in algorithms resulting from the use of unrepresentative training data are also needed to avoid biases that appear in AI's recommendation. Including in the governance mechanism of AI tools oriented toward making it credible and effective on healthcare is indispensable.

Funding for digital infrastructure and technological literacy needs to be studied as an integral part of a strategic approach to democratizing health information. To expand access to AI powered health tools in low resource environments, investments in digital infrastructure — reliable internet connectivity, and affordable devices — are required. At the same time, the maximization of adoption, and hence impact, requires initiatives to increase technological literacy for users. Government collaborations with technology companies and healthcare organizations can promote the deployment of large scale and sustainable solutions tackling infrastructural gaps and creating universal health access. Moreover, the democratization of health information aligns with the broader objectives of achieving the quadruple aim in healthcare: to improve patient outcomes, patient and provider experiences, reduce costs, and to promote equity. If AI tools are integrated into routine healthcare practices as a line of business, systems can standardize care delivery, eliminate inefficiencies, and provide data powered decision making to both stakeholders. It is this holistic approach that makes sure that healthcare is both more accessible and more inclusive and patient cantered.

Finally, we bring democratizing health information with AI tools to the fore as a major shift in healthcare delivery cantered on accessibility, inclusivity and patient empowerment. While traditional healthcare and healthcare systems in developing countries remain challenging, there are many innovative applications for AI including chatbots, wearables and personalized learning platforms to bridge healthcare access gaps, improve health literacy and promote a proactive form of care. Although it would be great to create this vision, it will not come without building solutions for ethical, infrastructural and governance issues to ensure equitable and sustainable implementation. Through its continued evolution AI will play a pivotal role in shaping the future of healthcare systems, in order to realize universal health coverage and better the quality of life for people all over the world.

5.3.3 Shared Decision-Making in Patient Care

Shared decision making (SDM) in patient care is a fundamental shift from person centred patient care to a collaboration between patients and patient care providers. The incorporation of the best available scientific evidence into the patient's values, preferences and goals in making informed healthcare decisions is this approach. It goes a step further from the traditional paternalistic model, in which clinicians take unilateral decisions on treatment pathways to partnership and dialogue. Through this collaborative process patients have an active role in making decisions around their health and in this case, promotes autonomy and shared responsibility of outcome (Montori et al., 2023).

When there are multiple treatment choices and risks and benefits, SDM is useful. SDM gives balanced information to patients which help them making decisions on what suits their believes and lifestyle. This includes medical evidence expertise, opinion of likely outcomes, and risks of the procedure, along with patient perspective of own values and life circumstances. The dynamic interplay between patients and healthcare providers improves healthcare interventions alignment to individual needs as well as promotes mutual respect between patients and providers (Hoque, 2024). The evidence suggests that SDM results in improved health outcomes, higher patient satisfaction, greater adherence to chosen treatments by people who have actively helped to design them. Several aspects concerning open communication, trust and the applying of decision aids in ESDM are important. SDM is a communication-based method, in which clinicians need to explain to patient's complex medical information in a concise, clear and understandable manner for patients, meanwhile listening during communication with patients. Trust is just as important because patients will collaborate more in making decisions with their provider when they feel they are empathetic and competent. Pamphlets, videos, interactive online tools and other decision aids, present evidence-based information about treatment options in an unbiased manner, playing a supporting role in helping people make decisions. These tools allow patients to understand and be prepared for, conversations with doctors (Marinkovic et al., 2022).

Given the strong benefits of implementing SDM, many challenges prevent the actual implementation. One major barrier is time constraints in crowded clinical settings which restrict the depth of conversation needed for the best decision making. Also, patients have different levels of health literacy and numeracy that can lead to having varying ability to understand, make sense of and weigh medical information. For their part, these barriers will have their own tailored answer: simplifying medical language, use visual aids, and embedding cultural sensitivity into the decision-making procedure. In addition, overcoming systemic obstacles will require sufficient training of healthcare professionals, and integration of SDM into routine workflows.

A second large challenge is the possibility of unequal power relationships between patients and providers. Now and then, patients may be reluctant to challenge their clinician's recommendations or voice contra opinions because they are perceived to be in an authority imbalance. To overcome this, clinicians must move to a facilitative role—encouraging questions, creating an inclusive environment where patients feel like they are valued and highly respected. To do this means developing interpersonal skills, like active listening and empathy in addition to technical and domain expertise. The use of structured communication frameworks, such as the SHARE approach, can further enhance the quality of SDM by guiding providers through sequential steps: To help the patient seek the patient's participation, explore options, assess values, reach a consensus, and evaluate outcomes.

The potential of SDM has, however, been increased by technological advancements through digital tools and telemedicine platforms. Digital health applications support patients with access to tailored information, monitor their health and provide remote engagement with providers as a means of encouraging informed discussions. AI driven decision aids can analyze patient data to give them personalized therapy suggestions that clinicians can incorporate in their decision. Telemedicine also offers SDM to rural or underprivileged people and ensures fair decision making. A patient's privacy has to be protected, and algorithm driven insights have to be accurate, these technologies have to be used with protections.

The SDM is important to respect patient autonomy and to promote beneficence, as the ethical underpinnings of SDM. By ensuring that patients know how much informed consent is needed in their care (the risks, benefits and uncertainties) SDM upholds the principle of informed consent. It also fits with the larger objectives of patient cantered care, focused on patient wellbeing and dignity. There are important ethical challenges to face including how to deal with when patients' preferences diverge from evidence-based recommendations. Although clinicians are obliged to provide high quality care, they also administer to a practical goal of respecting the welfare of patients by means of transparent and empathetic communication (Bae, 2017).

Finally, shared decision making is an important element of modern patient cantered care, one in which the patient and provider work together in partnership, with trust, and with mutual respect. But its benefits are not just healthier patients — it also increases patient empowerment and satisfaction. Yet despite the potential of SDM, time, health literacy, and power dynamics are all barriers to realizing the full potential of SDM, and technological innovations can play a central role in bolstering access and efficiency. In healthcare systems, SDM will be essential to delivering personalized, equitable and high-quality care as healthcare systems evolve.

5.4 Long-Term Vision for AI in Healthcare

In the long haul, artificial intelligence (AI) has the possibility to change how healthcare is practiced by boosting the further development of clinical practices, patient results and healthcare system proficiency. This vision rests on the fundamental ability of AI to be embedded in numerous healthcare applications and to form the foundation of precision medicine, efficient resource utilisation and greater accessibility for care. Finally, the path towards AI augmented systems is expected to set in for a paradigm shift from healthcare delivery that is increasingly patient centric, adaptive, and scalable. One of the most promising applications of AI over the long term will be in healthcare with precision medicine. AI can analyze large datasets that include genetic information, environmental factors and lifestyle information, and develop unique treatment plan for each patient. In oncology, in particular, this capacity to create personalized healthcare regimens is very important, as AI tools are already being used to predict tumor response to particular therapies helping to optimize treatment pathways and reduce adverse effects with the treatments in question. In the future, advancements in AI driven genomics and pharmacogenomics could permit future clinicians to identify at risk populations and initiated preventative interventions proactively, rather than reactively (Bajwa et al., 2021).

Another important part of its long-term vision involves integrating AI into clinical decision-making processes. With growing power, decision support systems based on AI are able to increasingly aggregate medical records, diagnostic imaging, and clinical data in order to support healthcare providers in making evidence-based decisions. AI models in diagnostics have already shown great promise in such systems, achieving accuracy levels comparable or above human experts in radiology, dermatology and pathology. In addition to reducing the risk of diagnostic error, these advancements increase the speed of diagnosis in stroke and myocardial infarction (Bohr & Memarzadeh, 2020; Salam & N, 2024). AI will also transform healthcare operations in streamlining them. This allows healthcare professional to give more of their time to patient care by automating administrative tasks such as scheduling and billing and medical documentation. With AI, AI powered predictive analytics can also efficiently manage hospital resources by forecasting patient admission, bed occupancy ratios and staff demands. We expect the deployment of AI for resource allocation to eventually reduce healthcare costs, while maintaining or improving care quality, and meet a critical challenge of healthcare systems around the world.

The idea of patient empowerment is a central theme of AI's long-term vision for healthcare. Real time health metrics monitoring is enabled by wearable devices and mobile applications interfaced with AI algorithms to let patients know what they are doing right or wrong in terms of their well-being. The versatility of this technology allows for early detection of anomalies, for early medical intervention. Additionally, AI driven health education and custom recommendations give the individuals an ability to make healthy decisions through the use of AI driven tools. These innovation plays a role in shifting from reactive to preventative care, and hence to lead a healthier life and to take off load from healthcare infrastructure (Reddy, 2024).

The long-term benefits of adopting such AI technologies will help solve the discontents of healthcare access. AI augmented telemedicine platforms can reach out to underserved regions, dismissing geographical barriers and resource shortcomings. With AI based language processing systems, communication can take place between different kinds of populations, making healthcare delivery inclusive. Furthermore, generative AI, the ability to generate and synthesize medical content, could also be majorly helpful in training healthcare workers to be upskilled and capable of providing high quality care in remote areas. In the coming years, to realize AI's long term potential in healthcare, many challenges will have to be addressed. If we are to continue to build and trust applications of AI, ethical considerations related to data privacy, algorithmic bias, informed consent need be at the forefront.

In addition, we will need to be able to develop interoperable systems able to merge multiple data sources in order to fully realize what AI has to offer. To establish the safe, robust in the healthcare using AI, it is necessary to collaborate with policymakers, technologists and healthcare providers to develop mutual, robust regulatory framework. Finally, AI will change and empower healthcare. Increased precision medicine, simplified operations, giving power to people, and making healthcare more accessible are all things AI could potentially do to revolutionise global healthcare. To use AI for sustainable and equitable health care we need innovation, ethical stewardship and collaborative governance.

5.4.1 AI as a Universal Health Enabler

The healthcare sector has been making extensive use of Artificial Intelligence (AI) as a powerful tool that increasingly contributes to the diversification of UHC. Being able to optimize medical service delivery and improve health outcomes, AI will be able to bridge large gaps in access and quality of medical service delivery; especially in poorly endowed and remote areas. The most attractive aspect of AI in health care is the capability of providing precision and consistency in care giving, which is critical in the situation where the resources of health care are scarce or unevenly distributed. If enabled, AI can be used to facilitate attend to diagnosis, make treatment recommendations, and assist in patient management globally, leading to better functioning of health centers, all around the world and therefore helping people get access to high quality care. Timely, evidence-based insights based on the best available AI are essential in supporting healthcare professionals to make clinical decisions. AI is able to evaluate enormous quantities of medical data including patient histories, medical imaging, and genetic information, and make more accurate predictions of disease progression, diagnosis and treatment outcomes, through advanced algorithms. This technology facilitates informed decisions from healthcare providers quickly with little to no errors at the expense of human safety in patients. In countries where medical expertise is rare, AI powered tool can be adjunct to medical practice, assuring patients appropriate care even when the actual medical expertise is missing. For instance, AI can use medical images at the same level of accuracy as (if not better than) trained radiologists to interpret them, greatly speeding up diagnosis and making it more widely accessible (Bold et al., 2023).

Additionally, AI is shaping up the health care delivery as personalized medicine, this focuses on treating the patients individually with their data. AI can help craft treatment which is tailored specifically for the person by analysing genetic, environmental and lifestyle factors. With this, we move towards precision medicine to avoid drug adverse reactions to improve therapeutic efficacy, given the challenge of chronic and complex disease care requiring continuous monitoring. AI enabled personalized approaches to long term condition management that have contributed to improving overall health outcomes and equitable delivery of care to all populations (Martinez-Millana et al., 2022). All these new developments in the use of AI in healthcare also have the potential to usher in the use of AI in the prevention and promotion of disease. These days, machine learning algorithms are predicting outbreaks of disease, tracking health trends, and monitoring conditions related to public health that affect the environment. Detected early signs of epidemics or the spread of infectious diseases can be by analysing big data from various sources, where pieces of data from all sources are put together to give AI so that we can have a "a bird's eye view". If implemented, these predictive capabilities can help health authorities respond with timely interventions, slow down the spread of disease and better use resources. AI solutions have made an impact in tracking and predicting the spread of COVID-19 and in helping governments decide based on data on lockdowns, resource distribution and vaccination campaigns.

Furthermore, in remote and underserved areas, AI facilitates healthcare access. As telemedicine is on the rise, AI based diagnostic tools could help support healthcare delivery in areas that might not have specialists. Here, an example is how AI enabled mobile application can help to diagnose the condition of skin cancer or diabetic retinopathy, thereby helping the people residing in remote areas to get consultations and diagnosis without travelling long distances. Consequently, AI provides access to healthcare for those outside geographical and socioeconomic barriers. Even more importantly, virtual medical translation through AI tools turns language and cultural barriers into a benefit; whether we're talking about a patient who isn't a native speaker or a minority population that is not well served by nearby healthcare providers, AI tools provide translation services that deliver accurate and timely medical care to all. The aspect of AI that we propose here coincides with global health goals such as universal health coverage (Gordon et al., 2024), assuming that health care delivery remains unequal. Besides being applied in the clinical field, AI has been impacting on healthcare administration and management. Through AI algorithms, operations can be streamlined, resource allocation can be optimised and patients can be predicting in flow to make hospitals more operational effective. For example, an AI system can read patient data to predict peak admission periods in order to prepare for the surges in demand for healthcare facilities. The efficiencies improve patient care and mitigate the financial burden on the systems providing health services making health services sustainable. With AI development, its role will not only be important in operational efficiency, wait time, and cost minimization in order to reach UHC goals globally (Okada et al., 2023).

Though this presents very promising applications, the integration of AI into healthcare systems has not been realised in the vast majority of applications. Data privacy concerns, the desire for sound regulatory regimes, and a fear that if AI technologies are not equitably distributed that current inequalities will be amplified. Along with this, however, AI's success depends on a workforce with the skills to sort through and make sense of complicated data, which requires contributions towards education and training. While appropriate safeguards and infrastructure can be built around AI to make it a transformative force in global healthcare which will increase universal health coverage and enhance the health outcomes of varied populations. Finally, AI is a strong enabler of universal health coverage because it brings solutions for increased access, efficiency, quality of care. It's also changing the healthcare landscape by supporting personalized medicine, making diseases easier to predict and prevent, and improving healthcare accessibility. But its integration has to be done carefully so that the benefits of AI do not fall upon the more privileged, and so that issues of data privacy and labour preparedness are dealt with as well. As we continue to innovate and implement, AI will be central in reaching the goal of universal health coverage globally through bettering both the delivery of healthcare and public health outcome.

5.4.2 Bridging Technology and Humanity in Medicine

Technology and humanity in the medical field is an unfolding story of how technology and humanism intersect. As healthcare systems navigate digital transformation, artificial intelligence and digital health tools, the imperative to strike the balance between technological innovation and empathy, compassion and patient autonomy becomes ever more primary. Technology in healthcare is certainly not about replacing human interaction; it's about taking what we already have and making it better in order to help patients and improve the quality of care. In particular, we have seen that AI can improve diagnostics, personalise treatment plans and predict health risks, but we need to be careful it doesn't overshadow the human touch we need in patient care. AI is growing into healthcare, as a perfect example of technology bridging the gap between efficiency and empathy. With AI driven systems, such as the analysis of large datasets, the identification of patterns, providing recommendations that support medical decision making. For instance, AI tools have been used to more accurately and faster that human doctors can detect diseases such as cancer. Not only does this make staff more efficient, it also prevents healthcare providers from spending so much time focused on direct patient interaction of building rapport and trust. Yet AI is also a double-edged sword. Supporting medical practitioners by automating routine tasks sounds good, but it questions human judgment and compassion in diagnosis and treatment and loss. In healthcare, we face the spectre between the efficiency of the AI and the human ability that ethnically and emotionally is to connect with patients.

Technology humanisation in healthcare is the development of systems that centre care around the patient. We then take this approach and extend how we think about healthcare, accounting for the emotional, psychological and social facets of healthcare that can get lost in purely technical applications. Digital health tools built in a human cantered design ensure that they are intuitive, accessible, and supportive of the relationship between doctor and patient. For example, AI systems can be made to deliver patients with simple, communicable information about their health conditions so that they can also engage themselves accordingly in deciding their care. Wearable devices further and health apps also facilitate patient's monitoring of health status and enable better communication between patients and healthcare provider, increasing the awareness in care process of patients. This use of technology to facilitate a shift in healthcare model towards personalized medicine has allowed the healthcare to become more proactive and patient driven, while creating a higher level of control and ownership of one's own health. The ethical considerations also need to be considered as we begin to bridge technology and humanity in medicine. As AI, big data and automation get more prevalent in healthcare, privacy, security and the biases in algorithms are concerns. One example is that if the input to an AI system is unbalanced (e.g. incomplete or biased), then AI systems trained on those data could make unfair recommendations of treatment, for instance, leading to unfair treatment for underrepresented populations. Failure to mitigate such risks require an implementation and development of AI based on ethical frameworks. Furthermore, there are moral implications of who owns the data, and what to do with sensitive health information. Yet, as healthcare systems strive to digitize, they must also begin to make patient consent, data security, and transparency a priority; that technology is used to the patient's advantage and in the right manner.

Conversely, telemedicine has also taken root as a critical technological answer to the problem of connecting healthcare providers and patients, especially in underserved or rural communities. It is telemedicine, which includes virtual consultations where the patients receive care from their homes without the barriers like the geographical distance, transportation cost and long waiting time. The pandemic has made the in-person consultations difficult but this digital health innovation has quickly become particularly vital. By depicting the potential power of technology to increase access to healthcare and to improve patient outcomes, in particular, for people who usually have a harder time getting traditional healthcare services, telemedicine shines. This digital model is extremely powerful, but it still needs to be closely integrated with in person care to foster the human connection necessary for good treatment.

This has also seen the rise of the concept of "Digital Health Humanities". This interdisciplinary approach combines humanities and digital technology and studies how the use of technology affects the human health and wellbeing. This highlights the need of human experience in health technology design and application. Meanwhile, as healthcare evolves, we need to think not just about how technically capable new systems are – but also how they will affect patients and healthcare providers socially and emotionally. At the same time, keeping healthcare holistically compassionate and focused on the patient is ensured by this approach to the upcoming technological innovations. With regards to patient care, technology is becoming less invasive and more supportive. The goal is to build a healthcare system that enhances and does not replace the care giving process with technology. One example of AI tools intended to help in remote patient monitoring and personalised treatment plans are aimed at supplementing, not replacing, the job of healthcare providers. That means patients still get the emotional and psychological support they need to be well while reaping the efficiencies technology can bring. But technology has made telemedicine more possible, and robotics has made it easier for specialists to connect with patients in real-time, all of which support the idea that technology should not be in the way of connecting humans, it should be to streamline humans. Finally, bridging technology and humanity in medicine is neither about choosing one over the other, but about making technology and humanity subservient to each other. Using AI and other digital tools hand in hand with healthcare providers to create better, more personalized care is the future of healthcare. The goal is to build a new, innovative and compassionate healthcare system that uses technology to empower doctors and patients to cooperate more, get better outcomes, and have a better patient experience.

5.4.3 Strategic Roadmap for Sustainable Growth

To achieve long term success in healthcare, strategic roadmap to sustainable growth is imperative to balance environmental, social and economic factors. Well planned approach balances operational efficiency and responsible practices of evolving landscape where there are continued increase in healthcare demands, regulatory pressures and financial constraint. This roadmap should incorporate equally the care of the patient as well as the responsible use of resources, energy conservation and equitable outcome of the health. Sustainable practices in the healthcare systems are adopted as a holistic process which begins with the technological advancement and to enhance the usage of resources, promoting community partnership as well as enforcing policies conformed to environmental, social and governance (ESG) criteria. A sound health care delivery system needs innovative models to support a comprehensive analysis that includes a sustainable growth strategy. From this perspective, hospitals must formulate and execute patient orientation, community participation and operational excellence strategies. These strategies must have patient care as their core, while operational practices should cut waste, reduce energy, and conserve resources in a responsible way. In light of potentially damaging climate change related to current global health infrastructure, this is particularly important. According to studies, hospitals that adopt green and energy efficient practices are not only doing the right thing by being more sustainable but are also making long term cost savings and improving patient outcomes through a cleaner healthier environment.

Both healthcare organizations and patients care about the environment – making the movement toward sustainability a proactive obligation. Environmental sustainability could be achieved through the use of renewable energy sources; waste reduction; improving energy efficiency. By implementing green building practices, healthcare organizations can cut its carbon footprints, optimize waste management system and use digital technologies to improve its operation. Hospitals should also strive to increase social equity by providing social equity access for underserved communities within hospitals and for all. Emphasis on sustainability can reduce the risk associated with environmental changes to healthcare systems and protect the wellbeing of future generations. A second major pillar of the strategic roadmap is to foster partnerships and alliance with external stakeholders.

With companies, government agencies, community groups, and other healthcare providers, these partnerships can range from working with technology providers. Through these collaborations healthcare organizations can learn from each other, find funding for sustainability initiatives, and make a transition to a more complete data system. Innovation also comes from collaboration in order for hospitals to find new ways to cut costs and improve patient care. Involving local community in designing and delivering health services adds to sustain healthcare initiatives. When hospitals align their goals with community health needs, they can produce long lasting value and trust which are critical to maintaining a sustainable healthcare ecosystem.

But strategic growth also means the healthcare industry needs to be looking at long term financial sustainability. In order to achieve its sustainability goals, hospitals must be able to manage their resources efficiently because doing so will help them stay financially viable. Effective resource allocation, supply chain management optimization, and collaboration with cost saving innovations like telemedicine and AI driven diagnostics, can all do the trick. In addition, data analytics integration into healthcare operations can allow hospitals to better predict demand, manage patient flow and reduce operations inefficiencies. These advancements not only help to meet environmental goals, but they also help to enhance the bottom line by reducing waste and facilitating a faster service delivery (Huebner & Flessa, 2022)dynamics and uncertainty of the system's regimes and the resulting need for strategic thinking in a long-term period. The scientific discussion of this issue is the aim of the present analytical framework. The starting point is the definition of the term strategic management itself, followed by a reflection on the requirements resulting from the changes in the political, social and economic value systems of our post-industrial society. In this context, Dynaxity Zone III is used to explain the long-term perspective, the high levels of complexity and uncertainty and the responsibility of strategic management as important parameters. For a practical illustration, we demonstrate two selected applications (German hospital financing systems and development process of implants. ESG frameworks are becoming increasingly important in incorporating into the strategic management of healthcare organizations. Healthcare providers can join the race to promote environmental stewardship and social responsibility and transparent governance through their growth strategies so that they can circle the goals of global sustainability. ESG integration into strategic decision making enables hospitals to assess risks, exploit opportunities and build an enduring, sustainable and resilient healthcare system. Moreover, ESG incorporates acts that will make the public image of the hospital better; enhance the satisfaction of the patients; and finally, increase the financial outcome of the hospital by attracting investments from socially responsible investors. Additionally, an effective strategic roadmap can only be implemented with robust lead ship and governance. Healthcare leadership needs to grow financially, but also develop a vision for sustainability. This includes doing with environmental and social outcomes top of mind, creating an innovation culture, and establishing a culture of sustainability company wide. To make sustainability part of the hospital's culture and operations, leaders need to engage stakeholders all levels, including employees, patients and local community. As we continue to develop our sustainability efforts as well as progress toward our sustainability goals, it is just as important to keep our stakeholders aligned with these efforts through transparent reporting on sustainability efforts and progress.

Finally, a strategic road map for sustainable development in healthcare is about building a healthcare ecosystem that is robust, inclusive, and responsive to both present and future issues, not only about improving operational efficiencies. Healthcare facilities may provide a basis for sustainable development that not only satisfies current requirements but also gets them ready for future uncertainty by combining environmental care, social fairness, and responsible government. Hospitals can guarantee their position as pioneers in the worldwide trend towards more sustainable healthcare delivery by welcoming innovation, creating alliances, and guaranteeing financial sustainability.

BIBLIOGRAPHY

A. Torad, M., & H. Hossamel-din, Y. (2021). Smart ambulance using IoT for blood transfer facilities. *Indonesian Journal of Electrical Engineering and Computer Science*. https://doi.org/10.11591/ijeecs.v22.i1.pp97-103

Abouelmehdi, K., Beni-Hessane, A., & Khaloufi, H. (2018). Big healthcare data: preserving security and privacy. *Journal of Big Data*. https://doi.org/10.1186/s40537-017-0110-7

Aerts, A., & Bogdan-Martin, D. (2021). Leveraging data and AI to deliver on the promise of digital health. *International Journal of Medical Informatics*. https://doi.org/10.1016/j.ijmedinf.2021.104456

Agarwal, V. (2015). Research on Data Preprocessing and Categorization Technique for Smartphone Review Analysis. *International Journal of Computer Applications*. https://doi.org/10.5120/ijca2015907309

Al Harbi, S., Aljohani, B., Elmasry, L., Baldovino, F. L., Raviz, K. B., Altowairqi, L., & Alshlowi, S. (2024). Streamlining patient flow and enhancing operational efficiency through case management implementation. *BMJ Open Quality*. https://doi.org/10.1136/bmjoq-2023-002484

Arora, G., Joshi, J., Mandal, R. S., Shrivastava, N., Virmani, R., & Sethi, T. (2021). Artificial intelligence in surveillance, diagnosis, drug discovery and vaccine development against covid-19. In *Pathogens*. https://doi.org/10.3390/pathogens10081048

Athanasopoulou, K., Daneva, G. N., Adamopoulos, P. G., & Scorilas, A. (2022). Artificial Intelligence: The Milestone in Modern Biomedical Research. In *BioMedInformatics*. https://doi.org/10.3390/biomedinformatics2040049

Author, P. (2011). How Many Friends Does One Person Need? Dunbar's Number and Other Evolutionary Quirks. *Mankind Quarterly*. https://doi.org/10.46469/mq.2011.51.4.5

Avanzo, M., Wei, L., Stancanello, J., Vallières, M., Rao, A., Morin, O., Mattonen, S. A., & El Naqa, I. (2020). Machine and deep learning methods for radiomics. *Medical Physics.* https://doi.org/10.1002/mp.13678

Bae, J. M. (2017). Shared decision making: relevant concepts and facilitating strategies. *Epidemiology and Health.* https://doi.org/10.4178/epih.e2017048

Bag, S., Wood, L. C., Xu, L., Dhamija, P., & Kayikci, Y. (2020). Big data analytics as an operational excellence approach to enhance sustainable supply chain performance. *Resources, Conservation and Recycling.* https://doi.org/10.1016/j.resconrec.2019.104559

Bajwa, Munir, J., Nori, U., & Williams, A. (2021). Artificial intelligence in healthcare: transforming the practice of medicine. *Future Healthcare Journal, 8*(2), e188–e194. https://doi.org/10.7861/fhj.2021-0095

Bala, I., Pindoo, I. A., Mijwil, M. M., Abotaleb, M., & Yundong, W. (2024). Ensuring Security and Privacy in Healthcare Systems: A Review Exploring Challenges, Solutions, Future Trends, and the Practical Applications of Artificial Intelligence. *Jordan Medical Journal, 58*(2), 250–270. https://doi.org/10.35516/jmj.v58i2.2527

Banerjee, S., Alsop, P., Jones, L., & Cardinal, R. N. (2022). Patient and public involvement to build trust in artificial intelligence: A framework, tools, and case studies. In *Patterns.* https://doi.org/10.1016/j.patter.2022.100506

Bardhan, I., Chen, H., & Karahanna, E. (2020). Connecting systems, data, and people: A multidisciplinary research roadmap for chronic disease management. In *MIS Quarterly: Management Information Systems.* https://doi.org/10.25300/MISQ/2020/14644

Bates, D. W., Levine, D. M., Salmasian, H., Syrowatka, A., Shahian, D. M., Lipsitz, S., Zebrowski, J. P., Myers, L. C., Logan, M. S., Roy, C. G., Iannaccone, C., Frits, M. L., Volk, L. A., Dulgarian, S., Amato, M. G., Edrees, H. H., Sato, L., Folcarelli, P., Einbinder, J. S., … Mort, E. (2023). The Safety of Inpatient Health Care. *New England Journal of Medicine.* https://doi.org/10.1056/nejmsa2206117

Batko, K., & Ślęzak, A. (2022). The use of Big Data Analytics in healthcare. *Journal of Big Data.* https://doi.org/10.1186/s40537-021-00553-4

Bedington, A., Halcomb, E. F., McKee, H. A., Sargent, T., & Smith, A. (2024). Writing with generative AI and human-machine teaming: Insights and recommendations from faculty and students. *Computers and Composition.* https://doi.org/10.1016/j.compcom.2024.102833

Blomberg, S. N., Christensen, H. C., Lippert, F., Ersbøll, A. K., Torp-Petersen, C., Sayre, M. R., Kudenchuk, P. J., & Folke, F. (2021). Effect of Machine Learning on Dispatcher Recognition of Out-of-Hospital Cardiac Arrest during Calls to Emergency Medical Services: A Randomized Clinical Trial. *JAMA Network Open*. https://doi.org/10.1001/jamanetworkopen.2020.32320

Bohr, A., & Memarzadeh, K. (2020). The rise of artificial intelligence in healthcare applications. In *Artificial Intelligence in Healthcare*. https://doi.org/10.1016/B978-0-12-818438-7.00002-2

Bold, B., Lkhagvajav, Z., & Dorjsuren, B. (2023). Role of Artificial Intelligence in Achieving Universal Health Coverage: A Mongolian Perspective. In *Korean Journal of Radiology*. https://doi.org/10.3348/kjr.2023.0668

Bonamigo, A., Bernardes, P. M. M., Conrado, L. F., & Calado, R. D. (2023). Optimizing patient flow in emergency care units and lean healthcare. In *Innovation, Strategy, and Transformation Frameworks for the Modern Enterprise*. https://doi.org/10.4018/979-8-3693-0458-7.ch007

Brown, J. M., Campbell, J. P., Beers, A., Chang, K., Ostmo, S., Chan, R. V. P., Dy, J., Erdogmus, D., Ioannidis, S., Kalpathy-Cramer, J., & Chiang, M. F. (2018). Automated diagnosis of plus disease in retinopathy of prematurity using deep convolutional neural networks. *JAMA Ophthalmology*. https://doi.org/10.1001/jamaophthalmol.2018.1934

Byrsell, F., Claesson, A., Ringh, M., Svensson, L., Jonsson, M., Nordberg, P., Forsberg, S., Hollenberg, J., & Nord, A. (2021). Machine learning can support dispatchers to better and faster recognize out-of-hospital cardiac arrest during emergency calls: A retrospective study. *Resuscitation*. https://doi.org/10.1016/j.resuscitation.2021.02.041

Canali, S., Schiaffonati, V., & Aliverti, A. (2022). Challenges and recommendations for wearable devices in digital health: Data quality, interoperability, health equity, fairness. *PLOS Digital Health*, *1*(10), e0000104. https://doi.org/10.1371/journal.pdig.0000104

Capobianco, E. (2017). Systems and precision medicine approaches to diabetes heterogeneity: a Big Data perspective. *Clinical and Translational Medicine*. https://doi.org/10.1186/s40169-017-0155-4

Capraro, V., Lentsch, A., Acemoglu, D., Akgun, S., Akhmedova, A., Bilancini, E., Bonnefon, J.-F., Brañas-Garza, P., Butera, L., Douglas, K. M., Everett, J., Gigerenzer, G., Greenhow, C., Hashimoto, D., Holt-Lunstad, J., Jetten, J.,

Johnson, S., Longoni, C., Lunn, P., ... Viale, R. (2024). The Impact of Generative Artificial Intelligence on Socioeconomic Inequalities and Policy Making. *SSRN Electronic Journal.* https://doi.org/10.2139/ssrn.4666103

Castiglioni, I., Rundo, L., Codari, M., Di Leo, G., Salvatore, C., Interlenghi, M., Gallivanone, F., Cozzi, A., D'Amico, N. C., & Sardanelli, F. (2021). AI applications to medical images: From machine learning to deep learning. In *Physica Medica.* https://doi.org/10.1016/j.ejmp.2021.02.006

Chen, A., Liu, L., & Zhu, T. (2024). Advancing the democratization of generative artificial intelligence in healthcare: a narrative review. *Journal of Hospital Management and Health Policy, 8*, 12–12. https://doi.org/10.21037/jhmhp-24-54

Chen, J. Q., & Benusa, A. (2017). HIPAA security compliance challenges: The case for small healthcare providers. *International Journal of Healthcare Management.* https://doi.org/10.1080/20479700.2016.1270875

Chen, X., Wang, Y., Wang, Y., Qu, X., & Ma, X. (2021). Customized bus route design with pickup and delivery and time windows: Model, case study and comparative analysis. *Expert Systems with Applications.* https://doi.org/10.1016/j.eswa.2020.114242

Chrimes, D., Moa, B., Kuo, M. H., & Kushniruk, A. (2017). Operational efficiencies and simulated performance of big data analytics platform over billions of patient records of a hospital system. *Advances in Science, Technology and Engineering Systems.* https://doi.org/10.25046/aj020104

Da Silva, M., Horsley, T., Singh, D., Da Silva, E., Ly, V., Thomas, B., Daniel, R. C., Chagal-Feferkorn, K. A., Iantomasi, S., White, K., Kent, A., & Flood, C. M. (2022). Legal concerns in health-related artificial intelligence: a scoping review protocol. *Systematic Reviews.* https://doi.org/10.1186/s13643-022-01939-y

Dalakoti, M., Wong, S., Lee, W., Lee, J., Yang, H., Loong, S., Loh, P. H., Tyebally, S., Djohan, A., Ong, J., Yip, J., Ngiam, K. Y., & Foo, R. (2024). Incorporating AI into cardiovascular diseases prevention–insights from Singapore. *The Lancet Regional Health - Western Pacific, 48*, 101102. https://doi.org/10.1016/j.lanwpc.2024.101102

Dash, S., Shakyawar, S. K., Sharma, M., & Kaushik, S. (2019). Big data in healthcare: management, analysis and future prospects. *Journal of Big Data.* https://doi.org/10.1186/s40537-019-0217-0

Dave, M., & Patel, N. (2023). Artificial intelligence in healthcare and education. *British Dental Journal.* https://doi.org/10.1038/s41415-023-5845-2

de Araújo Novaes, M. (2019). Telecare within different specialties. In *Fundamentals of Telemedicine and Telehealth.* https://doi.org/10.1016/B978-0-12-814309-4.00010-0

Dieleman, J. L., Baral, R., Birger, M., Bui, A. L., Bulchis, A., Chapin, A., Hamavid, H., Horst, C., Johnson, E. K., Joseph, J., Lavado, R., Lomsadze, L., Reynolds, A., Squires, E., Campbell, M., DeCenso, B., Dicker, D., Flaxman, A. D., Gabert, R., ... Murray, C. J. L. (2016). US Spending on Personal Health Care and Public Health, 1996-2013. *JAMA, 316*(24), 2627. https://doi.org/10.1001/jama.2016.16885

Duncan, I. G. (2011). *Healthcare risk adjustment and predictive modeling.* Actex Publications.

Dwivedi, Y. K., Sharma, A., Rana, N. P., Giannakis, M., Goel, P., & Dutot, V. (2023). Evolution of artificial intelligence research in Technological Forecasting and Social Change: Research topics, trends, and future directions. *Technological Forecasting and Social Change.* https://doi.org/10.1016/j.techfore.2023.122579

Ejike Innocent Nwankwo, Ebube Victor Emeihe, Mojeed Dayo Ajcgbilc, Janct Aderonke Olaboye, & Chukwudi Cosmos Maha. (2024). AI in personalized medicine: Enhancing drug efficacy and reducing adverse effects. *International Medical Science Research Journal, 4*(8), 806–833. https://doi.org/10.51594/imsrj.v4i8.1453

Elendu, C., Amaechi, D. C., Elendu, T. C., Jingwa, K. A., Okoye, O. K., John Okah, M., Ladele, J. A., Farah, A. H., & Alimi, H. A. (2023). Ethical implications of AI and robotics in healthcare: A review. In *Medicine (United States).* https://doi.org/10.1097/MD.0000000000036671

Esteva, A., Kuprel, B., Novoa, R. A., Ko, J., Swetter, S. M., Blau, H. M., & Thrun, S. (2017). Dermatologist-level classification of skin cancer with deep neural networks. *Nature, 542*(7639), 115–118. https://doi.org/10.1038/nature21056

Estupiñán Ricardo, J., Leyva Vázquez, M. Y., Peñafiel Palacios, A. J., & El Assafiri Ojeda, Y. (2021). Intelligence and intellectual property artificial. *Universidad y Sociedad.*

Feld, A. D. (2005). The Health Insurance Portability and Accountability Act (HIPAA): Its broad effect on practice. In *American Journal of Gastroenterology*. https://doi.org/10.1111/j.1572-0241.2005.50621.x

Fleuren, L. M., Thoral, P., Shillan, D., Ercole, A., Elbers, P. W. G., Hoogendoorn, M., Gibbison, B., Klausch, T. L. T., Guo, T., Roggeveen, L. F., Swart, E. L., & Girbes, A. R. J. (2020). Machine learning in intensive care medicine: ready for take-off? In *Intensive Care Medicine*. https://doi.org/10.1007/s00134-020-06045-y

Frohnert, B. I., Webb-Robertson, B. J., Bramer, L. M., Reehl, S. M., Waugh, K., Steck, A. K., Norris, J. M., & Rewers, M. (2020). Predictive modeling of Type 1 diabetes stages using disparate data sources. *Diabetes*. https://doi.org/10.2337/db18-1263

García-Magariño, I., Sarkar, D., & Lacuesta, R. (2019). Wearable technology and mobile applications for healthcare. In *Mobile Information Systems*. https://doi.org/10.1155/2019/6247094

Gerke, S., Minssen, T., & Cohen, G. (2020). Ethical and legal challenges of artificial intelligence-driven healthcare. In *Artificial Intelligence in Healthcare*. https://doi.org/10.1016/B978-0-12-818438-7.00012-5

Gichoya, J. W., Banerjee, I., Bhimireddy, A. R., Burns, J. L., Celi, L. A., Chen, L. C., Correa, R., Dullerud, N., Ghassemi, M., Huang, S. C., Kuo, P. C., Lungren, M. P., Palmer, L. J., Price, B. J., Purkayastha, S., Pyrros, A. T., Oakden-Rayner, L., Okechukwu, C., Seyyed-Kalantari, L., ... Zhang, H. (2022). AI recognition of patient race in medical imaging: a modelling study. *The Lancet Digital Health*. https://doi.org/10.1016/S2589-7500(22)00063-2

Gordon, M., Daniel, M., Ajiboye, A., Uraiby, H., Xu, N. Y., Bartlett, R., Hanson, J., Haas, M., Spadafore, M., Grafton-Clarke, C., Gasiea, R. Y., Michie, C., Corral, J., Kwan, B., Dolmans, D., & Thammasitboon, S. (2024). A scoping review of artificial intelligence in medical education: BEME Guide No. 84. In *Medical Teacher*. https://doi.org/10.1080/0142159X.2024.2314198

Guk, K., Han, G., Lim, J., Jeong, K., Kang, T., Lim, E. K., & Jung, J. (2019). Evolution of wearable devices with real-time disease monitoring for personalized healthcare. In *Nanomaterials*. https://doi.org/10.3390/nano9060813

Haenssle, H. A., Fink, C., Schneiderbauer, R., Toberer, F., Buhl, T., Blum, A., Kalloo, A., Ben Hadj Hassen, A., Thomas, L., Enk, A., Uhlmann, L., Alt,

C., Arenbergerova, M., Bakos, R., Baltzer, A., Bertlich, I., Blum, A., Bokor-Billmann, T., Bowling, J., … Zalaudek, I. (2018). Man against Machine: Diagnostic performance of a deep learning convolutional neural network for dermoscopic melanoma recognition in comparison to 58 dermatologists. *Annals of Oncology*. https://doi.org/10.1093/annonc/mdy166

Hashimoto, D. A., Rosman, G., Rus, D., & Meireles, O. R. (2018). Artificial Intelligence in Surgery: Promises and Perils. In *Annals of Surgery*. https://doi.org/10.1097/SLA.0000000000002693

Hermes, S., Riasanow, T., Clemons, E. K., Böhm, M., & Krcmar, H. (2020). The digital transformation of the healthcare industry: exploring the rise of emerging platform ecosystems and their influence on the role of patients. *Business Research*. https://doi.org/10.1007/s40685-020-00125-x

Holman, H. R. (2020). The Relation of the Chronic Disease Epidemic to the Health Care Crisis. In *ACR Open Rheumatology*. https://doi.org/10.1002/acr2.11114

Hoque, F. (2024). Shared Decision-Making in Patient Care: Advantages, Barriers and Potential Solutions. *Journal of Brown Hospital Medicine*, *3*(4). https://doi.org/10.56305/001c.122787

Hosny, A., Parmar, C., Quackenbush, J., Schwartz, L. H., & Aerts, H. J. W. L. (2018). Artificial intelligence in radiology. In *Nature Reviews Cancer*. https://doi.org/10.1038/s41568-018-0016-5

Hossain, M. S., & Muhammad, G. (2016). Healthcare Big Data Voice Pathology Assessment Framework. *IEEE Access*. https://doi.org/10.1109/ACCESS.2016.2626316

Huang, T., Xu, H., Wang, H., Huang, H., Xu, Y., Li, B., Hong, S., Feng, G., Kui, S., Liu, G., Jiang, D., Li, Z.-C., Li, Y., Ma, C., Su, C., Wang, W., Li, R., Lai, P., & Qiao, J. (2023). Artificial intelligence for medicine: Progress, challenges, and perspectives. *The Innovation Medicine*. https://doi.org/10.59717/j.xinn-med.2023.100030

Huebner, C., & Flessa, S. (2022). Strategic Management in Healthcare: A Call for Long-Term and Systems-Thinking in an Uncertain System. *International Journal of Environmental Research and Public Health*. https://doi.org/10.3390/ijerph19148617

Iqbal, M. J., Iqbal, M. M., Ahmad, I., Alassafi, M. O., Alfakeeh, A. S., & Alhomoud, A. (2021). Real-Time Surveillance Using Deep Learning. *Security and Communication Networks*. https://doi.org/10.1155/2021/6184756

Janani, S. R., Subramanian, R., Karthik, S., & Vimalarani, C. (2023). Healthcare Monitoring using Machine Learning Based Data Analytics. *International Journal of Computers, Communications and Control*. https://doi.org/10.15837/ijccc.2023.1.4973

Janiesch, C., Zschech, P., & Heinrich, K. (2021). Machine learning and deep learning. *Electronic Markets*. https://doi.org/10.1007/s12525-021-00475-2

Javaid, M., Haleem, A., Rab, S., Pratap Singh, R., & Suman, R. (2021). Sensors for daily life: A review. In *Sensors International*. https://doi.org/10.1016/j.sintl.2021.100121

Jeon, M., Ko, J., & Cheoi, K. (2024). Enhancing Surveillance Systems: Integration of Object, Behavior, and Space Information in Captions for Advanced Risk Assessment. *Sensors*. https://doi.org/10.3390/s24010292

John Dian, F., Vahidnia, R., & Rahmati, A. (2020). Wearables and the Internet of Things (IoT), Applications, Opportunities, and Challenges: A Survey. *IEEE Access, 8*, 69200–69211. https://doi.org/10.1109/ACCESS.2020.2986329

Johnson, M., Albizri, A., Harfouche, A., & Fosso-Wamba, S. (2022). Integrating human knowledge into artificial intelligence for complex and ill-structured problems: Informed artificial intelligence. *International Journal of Information Management*. https://doi.org/10.1016/j.ijinfomgt.2022.102479

Kakandikar, G. M., & Nandedkar, V. M. (2020). Big Data in Healthcare: Technical Challenges and Opportunities. In *Studies in Big Data*. https://doi.org/10.1007/978-3-030-31672-3_5

Khalifa, M., & Albadawy, M. (2024). Using artificial intelligence in academic writing and research: An essential productivity tool. In *Computer Methods and Programs in Biomedicine Update*. https://doi.org/10.1016/j.cmpbup.2024.100145

Kim, H. S., Kim, E. J., & Kim, J. Y. (2023). Emerging Trends in Artificial Intelligence-Based Urological Imaging Technologies and Practical Applications. In *International Neurourology Journal*. https://doi.org/10.5213/inj.2346286.143

Kirişci, M. (2019). Comparison of artificial neural network and logistic regression model for factors affecting birth weight. *SN Applied Sciences, 1*(4), 378. https://doi.org/10.1007/s42452-019-0391-x

Koutsouleris, N., Hauser, T. U., Skvortsova, V., & De Choudhury, M. (2022). From promise to practice: towards the realisation of AI-informed mental health care. In *The Lancet Digital Health.* https://doi.org/10.1016/S2589-7500(22)00153-4

Lee, A., Orr, W., Johnson, W. G., Harb, J. I., & Henne, K. (2023). Barriers to regulating AI: Critical observations from a fractured field. In *Handbook of Critical Studies of Artificial Intelligence.* https://doi.org/10.4337/9781803928562.00044

Liu, Y., & Yeoh, J. K. W. (2021). Robust pixel-wise concrete crack segmentation and properties retrieval using image patches. *Automation in Construction.* https://doi.org/10.1016/j.autcon.2020.103535

Liu, Z., Wang, X., Lu, K., & Su, D. (2019). Automatic arrhythmia detection based on convolutional neural networks. In *Computers, Materials and Continua.* https://doi.org/10.32604/cmc.2019.04882

Lombardo, G. (2022). The AI industry and regulation: Time for implementation? In *Ethical Evidence and Policymaking: Interdisciplinary and International Research.* https://doi.org/10.56687/9781447363972-013

Maltoni, D., Cappelli, R., & Meuwly, D. (2017). Handbook of Biometrics for Forensic Science. *Springer.*

Manchadi, O., Ben-Bouazza, F. E., & Jioudi, B. (2023). Predictive Maintenance in Healthcare System: A Survey. *IEEE Access.* https://doi.org/10.1109/ACCESS.2023.3287490

Marinkovic, V., Rogers, H. L., Lewandowski, R. A., & Stevic, I. (2022). Shared Decision Making. *Intelligent Systems Reference Library.* https://doi.org/10.1007/978-3-030-79353-1_5

Martinez-Millana, A., Saez-Saez, A., Tornero-Costa, R., Azzopardi-Muscat, N., Traver, V., & Novillo-Ortiz, D. (2022). Artificial intelligence and its impact on the domains of universal health coverage, health emergencies and health promotion: An overview of systematic reviews. In *International Journal of Medical Informatics.* https://doi.org/10.1016/j.ijmedinf.2022.104855

Mehta, N., & Pandit, A. (2018). Concurrence of big data analytics and healthcare: A systematic review. In *International Journal of Medical Informatics*. https://doi.org/10.1016/j.ijmedinf.2018.03.013

Mendelson, D., & Mendelson, D. (2017). Legal protections for personal health information in the age of Big Data – a proposal for regulatory framework. *Ethics, Medicine and Public Health*. https://doi.org/10.1016/j.jemep.2017.02.005

Mirbabaie, M., Hofeditz, L., Frick, N. R. J., & Stieglitz, S. (2022). Artificial intelligence in hospitals: providing a status quo of ethical considerations in academia to guide future research. *AI and Society*. https://doi.org/10.1007/s00146-021-01239-4

Mohammad Amini, M., Jesus, M., Fanaei Sheikholeslami, D., Alves, P., Hassanzadeh Benam, A., & Hariri, F. (2023). Artificial Intelligence Ethics and Challenges in Healthcare Applications: A Comprehensive Review in the Context of the European GDPR Mandate. In *Machine Learning and Knowledge Extraction*. https://doi.org/10.3390/make5030053

Montori, V. M., Ruissen, M. M., Hargraves, I. G., Brito, J. P., & Kunneman, M. (2023). Shared decision-making as a method of care. *BMJ Evidence-Based Medicine*. https://doi.org/10.1136/bmjebm-2022-112068

Morandini, S., Fraboni, F., De Angelis, M., Puzzo, G., Giusino, D., & Pietrantoni, L. (2023). THE IMPACT OF ARTIFICIAL INTELLIGENCE ON WORKERS' SKILLS: UPSKILLING AND RESKILLING IN ORGANISATIONS. *Informing Science*. https://doi.org/10.28945/5078

N., R. (2019). Artificial intelligence and security. Security 4.0. In *Security & Future*.

Nenova, Z., & Shang, J. (2022). Chronic Disease Progression Prediction: Leveraging Case-Based Reasoning and Big Data Analytics. *Production and Operations Management*. https://doi.org/10.1111/poms.13532

Ngozi Samuel Uzougbo, Chinonso Gladys Ikegwu, & Adefolake Olachi Adewusi. (2024). International enforcement of cryptocurrency laws: Jurisdictional challenges and collaborative solutions. *Magna Scientia Advanced Research and Reviews*, *11*(1), 068–083. https://doi.org/10.30574/msarr.2024.11.1.0075

Nicholson, W., Ii, P., Bračič, A., Cohen, G., Eisenberg, R., Ford, R., Lawrence, M., Madison, M., Menell, P., Outterson, K., Van Overwalle, G., Roin, B., Sachs, R., Sherkow, J., & Skopek, J. (2016). Big Data, Patents, and the Future of Medicine. In *Cardozo Law Review*.

Nilius, H., Cuker, A., Haug, S., Nakas, C., Studt, J. D., Tsakiris, D. A., Greinacher, A., Mendez, A., Schmidt, A., Wuillemin, W. A., Gerber, B., Kremer Hovinga, J. A., Vishnu, P., Graf, L., Kashev, A., Sznitman, R., Bakchoul, T., & Nagler, M. (2023). A machine-learning model for reducing misdiagnosis in heparin-induced thrombocytopenia: A prospective, multicenter, observational study. *EClinicalMedicine*. https://doi.org/10.1016/j.eclinm.2022.101745

Nizamuddin, M. K., Raziuddin, S., Farheen, M., Atheeq, C., & Sultana, R. (2024). An MLP-CNN Model for Real-time Health Monitoring and Intervention. *Engineering, Technology & Applied Science Research*, *14*(4), 15553–15558. https://doi.org/10.48084/etasr.7684

OECD. (2019). Scoping the OECD AI Principles: Deliberations of the Expert Group on Artificial Intelligence at the OECD (AIGO). *OECD Digital Economy Papers*.

Okada, Y., Mertens, M., Liu, N., Lam, S. S. W., & Ong, M. E. H. (2023). AI and machine learning in resuscitation: Ongoing research, new concepts, and key challenges. In *Resuscitation Plus*. https://doi.org/10.1016/j.resplu.2023.100435

Olawade, D. B., Aderinto, N., Olatunji, G., Kokori, E., David-Olawade, A. C., & Hadi, M. (2024). Advancements and applications of Artificial Intelligence in cardiology: Current trends and future prospects. *Journal of Medicine, Surgery, and Public Health*, *3*, 100109. https://doi.org/10.1016/j.glmedi.2024.100109

Onitiu, D. (2023). Mark Findlay et al (eds), Regulatory Insights on Artificial Intelligence . *Edinburgh Law Review*. https://doi.org/10.3366/elr.2023.0818

Otten, M., Jagesar, A. R., Dam, T. A., Biesheuvel, L. A., Den Hengst, F., Ziesemer, K. A., Thoral, P. J., De Grooth, H. J., Girbes, A. R. J., François-Lavet, V., Hoogendoorn, M., & Elbers, P. W. G. (2024). Does Reinforcement Learning Improve Outcomes for Critically Ill Patients? A Systematic Review and Level-of-Readiness Assessment. In *Critical Care Medicine*. https://doi.org/10.1097/CCM.0000000000006100

Palanisamy, V., & Thirunavukarasu, R. (2019). Implications of big data analytics in developing healthcare frameworks – A review. In *Journal of King Saud University - Computer and Information Sciences*. https://doi.org/10.1016/j.jksuci.2017.12.007

Paranjape, K., Schinkel, M., & Nanayakkara, P. (2020). Short Keynote Paper: Mainstreaming Personalized Healthcare-Transforming Healthcare through

New Era of Artificial Intelligence. *IEEE Journal of Biomedical and Health Informatics.* https://doi.org/10.1109/JBHI.2020.2970807

Parnaby, J., & Towill, D. R. (2008). Seamless healthcare delivery systems. In *International Journal of Health Care Quality Assurance.* https://doi.org/10.1108/09526860810868201

Powers, C. A., Meyer, C. M., Roebuck, M. C., & Vaziri, B. (2005). Predictive modeling of total healthcare costs using pharmacy claims data: A comparison of alternative econometric cost modeling techniques. *Medical Care.* https://doi.org/10.1097/01.mlr.0000182408.54390.00

Powles, J., & Hodson, H. (2017). Google DeepMind and healthcare in an age of algorithms. *Health and Technology.* https://doi.org/10.1007/s12553-017-0179-1

Prins, B. P., Leitsalu, L., Pärna, K., Fischer, K., Metspalu, A., Haller, T., & Snieder, H. (2021). Advances in genomic discovery and implications for personalized prevention and medicine: Estonia as example. *Journal of Personalized Medicine.* https://doi.org/10.3390/jpm11050358

Qian, Y., Siau, K. L., & Nah, F. F. (2024). Societal impacts of artificial intelligence: Ethical, legal, and governance issues. *Societal Impacts.* https://doi.org/10.1016/j.socimp.2024.100040

Rajpurkar, P., Hannun, A. Y., Haghpanahi, M., Bourn, C., & Ng, A. Y. (2017). *Cardiologist-Level Arrhythmia Detection with Convolutional Neural Networks.*

Rane, N. L., Rane, J., Paramesha, M., & Kaya, Ö. (2024). Emerging trends and future research opportunities in artificial intelligence, machine learning, and deep learning. In *Artificial Intelligence and Industry in Society 5.0.* Deep Science Publishing. https://doi.org/10.70593/978-81-981271-1-2_6

Rao, P. K., Singh, S., Dey, A., Rawtani, D., & Parikh, G. (2023). Automated Fingerprint Identification System. In *Modern Forensic Tools and Devices: Trends in Criminal Investigation.* https://doi.org/10.1201/b16315-20

Razzak, M. I., Imran, M., & Xu, G. (2020). Big data analytics for preventive medicine. *Neural Computing and Applications.* https://doi.org/10.1007/s00521-019-04095-y

Reddy, S. (2024). Generative AI in healthcare: an implementation science informed translational path on application, integration and governance.

Implementation Science, 19(1), 27. https://doi.org/10.1186/s13012-024-01357-9

Rehman, A., Naz, S., & Razzak, I. (2022). Leveraging big data analytics in healthcare enhancement: trends, challenges and opportunities. *Multimedia Systems.* https://doi.org/10.1007/s00530-020-00736-8

Ren, G., & Krawetz, R. (2015). Applying computation biology and "big data" to develop multiplex diagnostics for complex chronic diseases such as osteoarthritis. In *Biomarkers.* https://doi.org/10.3109/135475 0X.2015.1105499

Rivera, L. F., Villegas, N. M., Jiménez, M., Tamura, G., Angara, P., & Müller, H. A. (2020). Towards continuous monitoring in personalized healthcare through digital twins. *CASCON 2019 Proceedings - Conference of the Centre for Advanced Studies on Collaborative Research - Proceedings of the 29th Annual International Conference on Computer Science and Software Engineering.*

Rowe, J. P., & Lester, J. C. (2020). Artificial Intelligence for Personalized Preventive Adolescent Healthcare. In *Journal of Adolescent Health.* https://doi.org/10.1016/j.jadohealth.2020.02.021

Sadoughi, F., Behmanesh, A., & Sayfouri, N. (2020). Internet of things in medicine: A systematic mapping study. In *Journal of Biomedical Informatics.* https://doi.org/10.1016/j.jbi.2020.103383

Salam, A., & N, A. (2024). Revolutionizing dermatology: The role of artificial intelligence in clinical practice. *IP Indian Journal of Clinical and Experimental Dermatology, 10*(2), 107–112. https://doi.org/10.18231/j.ijced.2024.021

Seera, M., & Lim, C. P. (2014). A hybrid intelligent system for medical data classification. *Expert Systems with Applications.* https://doi.org/10.1016/j.eswa.2013.09.022

Selvaraj, S. (2024). Empowering Patients with AI-Driven Personalized Care: The Transformative Power of Generative AI and Healthcare Data Integration. *International Journal of Science and Research (IJSR), 13*(7), 337–343. https://doi.org/10.21275/SR24703063340

Shamayleh, A., Awad, M., & Farhat, J. (2020). IoT Based Predictive Maintenance Management of Medical Equipment. *Journal of Medical Systems.* https://doi.org/10.1007/s10916-020-1534-8

Sharma, I., Karwasra, R., Akram, U., Suchal, K., & Singh, S. (2024). AI-Empowered Prediction of Prognosis and Treatment Response in Rheumatoid Arthritis. In *Studies in Computational Intelligence.* https://doi.org/10.1007/978-981-99-9029-0_13

Shelmerdine, S. C. (2024). Revolutionising paediatric radiology: the future impact of artificial intelligence. In *European Radiology.* https://doi.org/10.1007/s00330-023-10288-w

Shenoy, A., & Appel, J. M. (2017). Safeguarding confidentiality in electronic health records. *Cambridge Quarterly of Healthcare Ethics.* https://doi.org/10.1017/S0963180116000931

Shuford, J., & Islam, M. M. (2024). Exploring the Latest Trends in Artificial Intelligence Technology: A Comprehensive Review. *Journal of Artificial Intelligence General Science (JAIGS) ISSN:3006-4023*, *2*(1). https://doi.org/10.60087/jaigs.v2i1.p13

Singh, M. (2018). Revolutionizing healthcare through artificial intelligence and virtual reality. *International Journal of Education and Management Studies.*

Sonawani, S., Patil, K., & Natarajan, P. (2023). Biomedical signal processing for health monitoring applications: a review. *International Journal of Applied Systemic Studies.* https://doi.org/10.1504/IJASS.2021.10045116

Stamey, T. A., Barnhill, S. D., Zhang, Z., Madyastha, K. R., Prestigiacomo, A. F., Jones, K., & Chan, D. (1996). Effectiveness of ProstAsure in detecting prostate cancer (PCa) and benign prostatic hyperplasia (BPH) in men age 50 and older. *J Urol*, *155*(Suppl), 436A.

Steerling, E., Siira, E., Nilsen, P., Svedberg, P., & Nygren, J. (2023). Implementing AI in healthcare—the relevance of trust: a scoping review. In *Frontiers in Health Services.* https://doi.org/10.3389/frhs.2023.1211150

Strandberg-Larsen, M., & Krasnik, A. (2009). Measurement of integrated healthcare delivery: A systematic review of methods and future research directions. *International Journal of Integrated Care.* https://doi.org/10.5334/ijic.305

Subash Chandra Nayak. (2024). Smart Hospitals: Integrating AI for Enhanced Patient Outcomes. *Journal of Electrical Systems*, *20*(10s), 1812–1819. https://doi.org/10.52783/jes.5446

Tadiboina, S. N. (2022). The Use Of AI In Advanced Medical Imaging. *Journal of Positive School Psychology* .

Taherdoost, H., & Ghofrani, A. (2024). AI's role in revolutionizing personalized medicine by reshaping pharmacogenomics and drug therapy. *Intelligent Pharmacy*, *2*(5), 643–650. https://doi.org/10.1016/j.ipha.2024.08.005

Tai, M. C. T. (2020). The impact of artificial intelligence on human society and bioethics. *Tzu Chi Medical Journal*, *32*(4), 339–343. https://doi.org/10.4103/tcmj.tcmj_71_20

Talib, S. H., Abdul-Rahaim, L. A., Alrubaie, A. J., & Raseed, I. M. (2023). Design smart hospital system based on cloud computing. *Indonesian Journal of Electrical Engineering and Computer Science*. https://doi.org/10.11591/ijeecs.v29.i2.pp797-807

Terry, N. P. (2019). Of Regulating Healthcare AI and Robots. *SSRN Electronic Journal*. https://doi.org/10.2139/ssrn.3321379

Thoral, P. J., Fornasa, M., De Bruin, D. P., Tonutti, M., Hovenkamp, H., Driessen, R. H., Girbes, A. R. J., Hoogendoorn, M., & Elbers, P. W. G. (2021). Explainable Machine Learning on AmsterdamUMCdb for ICU Discharge Decision Support: Uniting Intensivists and Data Scientists. *Critical Care Explorations*. https://doi.org/10.1097/CCE.0000000000000529

Thoral, P. J., Peppink, J. M., Driessen, R. H., Sijbrands, E. J. G., Kompanje, E. J. O., Kaplan, L., Bailey, H., Kesecioglu, J., Cecconi, M., Churpek, M., Clermont, G., Van Der Schaar, M., Ercole, A., Girbes, A. R. J., & Elbers, P. W. G. (2021). Sharing ICU Patient Data Responsibly Under the Society of Critical Care Medicine/European Society of Intensive Care Medicine Joint Data Science Collaboration: The Amsterdam University Medical Centers Database (AmsterdamUMCdb) Example*. *Critical Care Medicine*. https://doi.org/10.1097/CCM.0000000000004916

Thorat, V., Rao, P., Joshi, N., Talreja, P., & Shetty, A. R. (2024). Role of Artificial Intelligence (AI) in Patient Education and Communication in Dentistry. *Cureus*. https://doi.org/10.7759/cureus.59799

Topol, E. (2019). Deep Medicine - How Artificial Intelligence Can Make Healthcare Human Again. In *Journal of Chemical Information and Modeling*.

Tuli, S., Tuli, S., Wander, G., Wander, P., Gill, S. S., Dustdar, S., Sakellariou, R., & Rana, O. (2020). Next generation technologies for smart healthcare:

challenges, vision, model, trends and future directions. In *Internet Technology Letters*. https://doi.org/10.1002/itl2.145

van de Sande, D., van Genderen, M. E., Huiskens, J., Gommers, D., & van Bommel, J. (2021). Moving from bytes to bedside: a systematic review on the use of artificial intelligence in the intensive care unit. In *Intensive Care Medicine*. https://doi.org/10.1007/s00134-021-06446-7

van Wijngaarden, J. D. H., de Bont, A. A., & Huijsman, R. (2006). Learning to cross boundaries: The integration of a health network to deliver seamless care. *Health Policy*. https://doi.org/10.1016/j.healthpol.2006.01.002

Verma, P., & Sood, S. K. (2018). Cloud-centric IoT based disease diagnosis healthcare framework. *Journal of Parallel and Distributed Computing*. https://doi.org/10.1016/j.jpdc.2017.11.018

Viceconti, M., Hunter, P., & Hose, R. (2015). Big Data, Big Knowledge: Big Data for Personalized Healthcare. *IEEE Journal of Biomedical and Health Informatics*. https://doi.org/10.1109/JBHI.2015.2406883

Viegi, G., Maio, S., Fasola, S., & Baldacci, S. (2020). Global Burden of Chronic Respiratory Diseases. *Journal of Aerosol Medicine and Pulmonary Drug Delivery*. https://doi.org/10.1089/jamp.2019.1576

Visibelli, A., Roncaglia, B., Spiga, O., & Santucci, A. (2023). The Impact of Artificial Intelligence in the Odyssey of Rare Diseases. In *Biomedicines*. https://doi.org/10.3390/biomedicines11030887

Walsh, C. G., Ribeiro, J. D., & Franklin, J. C. (2018). Predicting suicide attempts in adolescents with longitudinal clinical data and machine learning. *Journal of Child Psychology and Psychiatry and Allied Disciplines*. https://doi.org/10.1111/jcpp.12916

Wang, X., Liang, T., Li, J., Roy, S., Pandey, V., Du, Y., & Kong, J. (2021). Artificial Intelligence-Empowered Chatbot for Effective COVID-19 Information Delivery to Older Adults. *International Journal of E-Health and Medical Communications*. https://doi.org/10.4018/IJEHMC.293285

Wang, Y., Ge, X., Ma, H., Qi, S., Zhang, G., & Yao, Y. (2021). Deep Learning in Medical Ultrasound Image Analysis: A Review. *IEEE Access*. https://doi.org/10.1109/ACCESS.2021.3071301

Willemink, M. J., Koszek, W. A., Hardell, C., Wu, J., Fleischmann, D., Harvey, H., Folio, L. R., Summers, R. M., Rubin, D. L., & Lungren, M. P. (2020).

Preparing medical imaging data for machine learning. In *Radiology*. https://doi.org/10.1148/radiol.2020192224

Wills, M. J. (2014). Decisions through data: Analytics in healthcare. *Journal of Healthcare Management*. https://doi.org/10.1097/00115514-201407000-00005

Wilson, B. J., & Nicholls, S. G. (2015). The human genome project, and recent advances in personalized genomics. In *Risk Management and Healthcare Policy*. https://doi.org/10.2147/RMHP.S58728

Wojtak, A., Fleming, C., & Barraclough, F. (2019). A global review of current and emerging education and training to advance integrated systems of care. *International Journal of Integrated Care*. https://doi.org/10.5334/ijic.s3361

Wojtara, M., Rana, E., Rahman, T., Khanna, P., & Singh, H. (2023). Artificial intelligence in rare disease diagnosis and treatment. In *Clinical and Translational Science*. https://doi.org/10.1111/cts.13619

Zhan, A., Mohan, S., Tarolli, C., Schneider, R. B., Adams, J. L., Sharma, S., Elson, M. J., Spear, K. L., Glidden, A. M., Little, M. A., Terzis, A., Ray Dorsey, E., & Saria, S. (2018). Using smartphones and machine learning to quantify Parkinson disease severity the mobile Parkinson disease score. *JAMA Neurology*. https://doi.org/10.1001/jamaneurol.2018.0809

Zhang, L., Guo, W., & Lv, C. (2024). Modern technologies and solutions to enhance surveillance and response systems for emerging zoonotic diseases. *Science in One Health*, *3*, 100061. https://doi.org/10.1016/j.soh.2023.100061

Zhang, Y., Qiu, M., Tsai, C. W., Hassan, M. M., & Alamri, A. (2017). Health-CPS: Healthcare cyber-physical system assisted by cloud and big data. *IEEE Systems Journal*. https://doi.org/10.1109/JSYST.2015.2460747

Zimolzak, A. J., Wei, L., Mir, U., Gupta, A., Vaghani, V., Subramanian, D., & Singh, H. (2024). Machine Learning to Enhance Electronic Detection of Diagnostic Errors. *JAMA Network Open*, *7*(9), e2431982. https://doi.org/10.1001/jamanetworkopen.2024.31982

Zirar, A., Ali, S. I., & Islam, N. (2023). Worker and workplace Artificial Intelligence (AI) coexistence: Emerging themes and research agenda. *Technovation*. https://doi.org/10.1016/j.technovation.2023.102747